GRADES
5-6

...the Super Source®
Color Tiles

Cuisenaire Company of America, Inc.
White Plains, NY

Cuisenaire extends its warmest thanks to the many teachers and students across the country who helped ensure the success of the Super Source® series by participating in the outlining, writing, and field testing of the materials.

Project Director: Judith Adams
Managing Editor: Doris Hirschhorn
Editorial Team: John Nelson, Deborah J. Slade, Harriet Slonim, Linda Dodge, Patricia Kijak Anderson
Editorial Assistant: Toni-Ann Bleecker
Field Test Coordinator: Laurie Verdeschi

Design Manager: Phyllis Aycock
Text Design: Amy Berger, Tracey Munz
Line Art and Production: Joan Lee, Fiona Santoianni
Cover Design: Michael Muldoon
Illustrations: Sean Farrell

...the Super Source®
Table of Contents

Using the Super Source™

The Super Source™ is a series of books each of which contains a collection of activities to use with a specific math manipulative. Driving *the Super Source*™ is Cuisenaire's conviction that children construct their own understandings through rich, hands-on mathematical experiences. Although the activities in each book are written for a specific grade range, they all connect to the core of mathematics learning that is important to every K-6 child. Thus, the material in many activities can easily be refocused for children at other grade levels. Because the activities are not arranged sequentially, children can work on any activity at any time.

The lessons in *the Super Source*™ all follow a basic structure consistent with the vision of mathematics teaching described in the *Curriculum and Evaluation Standards for School Mathematics* published by the National Council of Teachers of Mathematics.

All of the activities in this series involve Problem Solving, Communication, Reasoning, and Mathematical Connections—the first four NCTM Standards. Each activity also focuses on one or more of the following curriculum strands: Number, Geometry, Measurement, Patterns/Functions, Probability/Statistics, Logic.

HOW LESSONS ARE ORGANIZED

At the beginning of each lesson, you will find, to the right of the title, both the major curriculum strands to which the lesson relates and the particular topics that children will work with. Each lesson has three main sections. The first, GETTING READY, offers an *Overview*, which states what children will be doing, and why, and a list of "What You'll Need." Specific numbers of Color Tiles are suggested on this list but can be adjusted as the needs of your specific situation dictate. Before an activity, tiles can be counted out and placed in containers or self-sealing plastic bags for easy distribution. When crayons are called for, it is understood that their colors are those that match the Color Tiles and that markers may be used in place of crayons. Blackline masters that are provided for your convenience at the back of the book are referenced on this list. Paper, pencils, scissors, tape, and materials for making charts, which are necessary in certain activities, are usually not.

Although overhead Color Tiles and the suggestion to make overhead transparencies of the blackline masters are always listed in "What You'll Need" as optional, these materials are highly effective when you want to demonstrate the use of Color Tiles. As you move the tiles on the screen, children can work with the same materials at their seats. Children can also use the overhead to present their work to other members of their group or to the class.

The second section, THE ACTIVITY, first presents a possible scenario for *Introducing* the children to the activity. The aim of this brief introduction is to help you give children the tools they will need to investigate independently. However, care has been taken to avoid undercutting the activity itself. Since these investigations are designed to enable children to increase their own mathematical power, the idea is to set the stage but not steal the show! The heart of the lesson, *On Their Own*, is found in a box at the top of the second page of each lesson. Here, rich problems stimulate many different problem-solving approaches and lead to a variety of solutions. These hands-on explorations have the potential for bringing children to new mathematical ideas and deepening skills.

On Their Own is intended as a stand-alone activity for children to explore with a partner or in a small group. Be sure to make the needed directions clearly visible. You may want to write them on the chalkboard or on an overhead or present them either on reusable cards or paper. For children who may have difficulty reading the directions, you can read them aloud or make sure that at least one "reader" is in each group.

The last part of this second section, *The Bigger Picture*, gives suggestions for how children can share their work and their thinking and make mathematical connections. Class charts and children's recorded work provide a springboard for discussion. Under "Thinking and Sharing," there are several prompts that you can use to promote discussion. Children will not be able to respond to these prompts with one-word answers. Instead, the prompts encourage children to describe what they notice, tell how they found their results, and give the reasoning behind their answers. Thus children learn to verify their own results rather than relying on the teacher to determine if an answer is "right" or "wrong." Though the class discussion might immediately follow the investigation, it is important not to cut the activity short by having a class discussion too soon.

The Bigger Picture often includes a suggestion for a "Writing" (or drawing) assignment. This is meant to help children process what they have just been doing. You might want to use these ideas as a focus for daily or weekly entries in a math journal that each child keeps.

From: *What Happens to the Area?*

From: *Border Tiles*

The Bigger Picture always ends with ideas for "Extending the Activity." Extensions take the essence of the main activity and either alter or extend its parameters. These activities are well used with a class that becomes deeply involved in the primary activity or for children who finish before the others. In any case, it is probably a good idea to expose the entire class to the possibility of, and the results from, such extensions.

The third and final section of the lesson is TEACHER TALK. Here, in *Where's the Mathematics?*, you can gain insight into the underlying mathematics of the activity and discover some of the strategies children are apt to use as they work. Solutions are also given—when such are necessary and/or helpful. Because *Where's the Mathematics?* provides a view of what may happen in the lesson as well as the underlying mathematical potential that may grow out of it, this may be the section that you want to read before presenting the activity to children.

USING THE ACTIVITIES

The Super Source™ has been designed to fit into the variety of classroom environments in which it will be used. These range from a completely manipulative-based classroom to one in which manipulatives are just beginning to play a part. You may choose to use some activities in **the Super Source™** in the way set forth in each lesson (introducing an activity to the whole class, then breaking the class up into groups that all work on the same task, and so forth). You will then be able to circulate among the groups as they work to observe and perhaps comment on each child's work. This approach requires a full classroom set of materials but allows you to concentrate on the variety of ways that children respond to a given activity.

Alternatively, you may wish to make two or three related activities available to different groups of children at the same time. You may even wish to use different manipulatives to explore the same mathematical concept. (Cuisenaire® Rods and Snap™ Cubes, for example, can be used to teach some of the same concepts as Color Tiles.) This approach does not require full classroom sets of a particular manipulative. It also permits greater adaptation of materials to individual children's needs and/or preferences.

If children are comfortable working independently, you might want to set up a "menu"— that is, set out a number of related activities from which children can choose. Children should be encouraged to write about their experiences with these independent activities.

However you choose to use **the Super Source™** activities, it would be wise to allow time for several groups or the entire class to share their experiences. The dynamics of this type of interaction, in which children share not only solutions and strategies but also feelings and intuitions, is the basis of continued mathematical growth. It allows children who are beginning to form a mathematical structure to clarify it and those who have mastered just isolated concepts to begin to see how these concepts might fit together.

Again, both the individual teaching style and combined learning styles of the children should dictate the specific method of utilizing **the Super Source™** lessons. At first sight, some activities may appear too difficult for some of your children, and you may find yourself tempted to actually "teach" by modeling exactly how an activity can lead to a particular learning outcome. If you do this, you rob children of the chance to try the activity in whatever way they can. As long as children have a way to begin an investigation, give them time and opportunity to see it through. Instead of making assumptions about what children will or won't do, watch and listen. The excitement and challenge of the activity—as well as the chance to work cooperatively—may bring out abilities in children that will surprise you.

If you are convinced, however, that an activity does not suit your students, adjust it, by all means. You may want to change the language, either by simplifying it or by referring to specific vocabulary that you and your children already use and are comfortable with. On the other hand, if you suspect that an activity is not challenging enough, you may want to read through the activity extensions for a variation that you can give children instead.

RECORDING

Although the direct process of working with Color Tiles is a valuable one, it is afterward, when children look at, compare, share, and think about their work, that an activity yields its greatest rewards. However, because Color Tile designs can't always be left intact, children need an effective way to record their work. To this end, at the back of this book recording paper is provided for reproduction. The "What You'll Need" listing at the beginning of each lesson often specifies the kind of recording paper to use. For example, it seems natural for children to record Color Tile patterns on grid paper. Yet it is important for children to use a method of recording that they feel comfortable with. Frustration in recording their structures can leave children feeling that the actual activity was either too difficult or just not fun! Thus, there may be times when you feel children should just share their work rather than record it.

From: _Hexominoes_

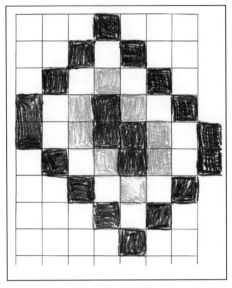

From: _Symmetry All Around_

Young children might duplicate their work on grid paper by coloring in boxes on grids that exactly match the tiles in size. Older children may be able to use smaller grids or even construct the recording paper as they see fit.

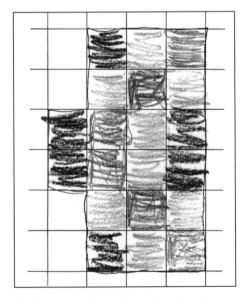

From: _How Does Your Garden Grow?_

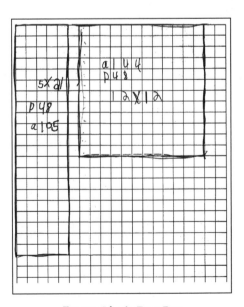

From: _Lisa's Dog Pen_

Color Tiles ◆ Grades 5-6 **7**

Another interesting way to "freeze" a Color Tile design is to create it using a software piece, and then get a printout. Children can use a classroom or resource-room computer if it is available or, where possible, extend the activity into a home assignment by utilizing their home computers.

Recording involves more than copying designs. Writing, drawing, and making charts and tables are also ways to record. By creating a table of data gathered in the course of their investigations, children are able to draw conclusions and look for patterns. When children write or draw, either in their group or later by themselves, they are clarifying their understanding of their recent mathematical experience.

Area	Perimiter
22	38
22	37
22	31
22	36
22	42
22	44
22	20
22	26
22	46
22	44

From: *Making Shapes*

# of Blue tiles = 9
# of Red tiles = 9
# of green tiles = 10
# of Yellow tiles = 8
                    36

Blue	Red	Green	Yellow
$\frac{9}{36} = \frac{1}{4}$	$\frac{9-1}{36-4}$	$\frac{10-5}{36\ 18}$	$\frac{8-2}{36\ 9}$

From: *Making Flags*

I used
# of People 14 6 tiles
16 7 tiles
20 9 tiles
50 24 tiles
100 56 tiles

I used different shapes to seat more people.

From: *Small Square Tables*

Design No.1	Real Tiles	Blue tiles	Total Tiles
1	2	2	4
2	2	3	5
3	2	4	6
4	2	5	7
1	4	4	8
2	5	8	13
3	6	12	18
10	13	40	53
15	18	60	78

From: *Patterns and Functions*

With a roomful of children busily engaged in their investigations, it is not easy for a teacher to keep track of how individual children are working. Having tangible material to gather and examine when the time is right will help you to keep in close touch with each child's learning.

Exploring Color Tiles

Color Tiles are a versatile collection of 1-inch square tiles which come in four colors—red, green, yellow, and blue. They are pleasant to handle and easy to manipulate. Children can use the tiles to act out story problems involving all sorts of everyday objects. Learning to use small colored squares to represent such objects is a significant step in the process of learning to abstract.

Although Color Tiles are simple in concept, they can be used to develop a wide variety of mathematical ideas at many different levels of complexity. Young children who start using Color Tiles to make patterns may be likely to talk about numbers of different-colored tiles. Some children may even spontaneously begin to count and compare numbers. The fact that the tiles are squares means that they fit naturally into a grid pattern, and when Color Tiles are used on top of a printed grid—for example, a number chart—the tiles can be used to discover many number patterns. As they record their patterns, children are also using their spatial skills and strategies to locate positions of particular tiles.

From: *Two-Thirds Blue*

When making patterns, children often provide the best inspiration for one another. Given sufficient time, some child will come up with an idea that excites the imagination of other children. It is preferable that new ideas arise in this way, because then children develop confidence in their own abilities to be creative. Though children need to explore patterns freely, some children may also appreciate challenges, such as being asked to make patterns with certain types of symmetry or patterns with certain characteristics, such as specific colors that represent different fractional parts.

Juan's idea was the most sensible because his idea took up less fensing and had more room for plants.

From: *How Does Your Garden Grow?*

Logical thinking is always involved when children investigate Color Tile patterns, because, in order to recognize and continue a visual pattern, children must form conjectures, verify them, and then apply them.

WORKING WITH COLOR TILES

As counters, Color Tiles are very important early number models. Eventually children will develop more abstract concepts of numbers and will not be dependent on manipulation of objects. Color Tiles can help children build such abstract structures.

The tiles fall naturally into certain patterns, as shown below, and enable children to visualize the relationships as represented by the tiles.

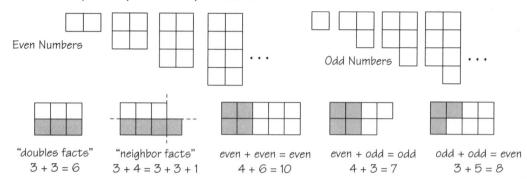

Even Numbers ... Odd Numbers ...

"doubles facts"
$3 + 3 = 6$

"neighbor facts"
$3 + 4 = 3 + 3 + 1$

even + even = even
$4 + 6 = 10$

even + odd = odd
$4 + 3 = 7$

odd + odd = even
$3 + 5 = 8$

Since there are large numbers of them, Color Tiles are useful for estimation and developing number sense. Children can take a handful, estimate how many, then separate the tiles into rows of ten to identify how many "tens" and how many "ones" there are. The colors of the tiles also make them useful in developing the concept of place value. For example, children can play exchange games in which each color tile represents a place value—ones, tens, hundreds, and thousands. Exchange games can work for subtraction as well as addition, and can also refer to decimals, where tile colors would represent units, tenths, hundredths, and thousandths.

Color Tiles are very suitable for developing an understanding of the meaning of addition. The sum 2 + 3 can be modeled by taking two tiles of one color and three of another, and then counting them. Subtraction problems can also be modeled either traditionally—put up five tiles and take two away—or by taking five tiles of one color, then covering two with a different color so that it is obvious that three tiles of the original color are left. Either of these methods of modeling makes the connection between addition and subtraction apparent.

Color Tiles are also ideal for developing the concept of multiplication, both as grouping and as an array. To show 3 x 4, children can make three groups with four tiles in each group and then arrange them in a rectangular array of three rows of four tiles. The advantage of the array is that by turning it children can see that 3 x 4 = 4 x 3. The array model also leads naturally into the development of the formula for the area of the rectangle. In fact, Color Tiles are especially suitable for exploring all area and perimeter relations.

Color Tiles can be used to explore all the different ways that squares can be arranged, subject to certain constraints. One classic investigation is to find all "tetraminoes," "pentominoes," and "hexominoes;" that is, all ways to arrange either four, five, or six tiles, respectively, so that one complete side of each tile touches at least one complete side of another tile. Color Tiles can be used to investigate how many different rectangular arrays a given number of tiles can have. This helps children to discover that for some numbers—prime numbers—the only possible rectangular arrays are one-tile wide. At an upper-grade level, the colors of tiles can represent prime numbers, and a set of tiles can be used to represent the prime factorization of a number. For example, if a red tile represents 2 and a green tile represents 3, the number 24 might be represented by three red tiles and one green tile, since 24 = 2 x 2 x 2 x 3. This representation of numbers in terms of factors can help children to understand procedures for finding greatest common divisors and least common multiples. Since the Color Tiles all feel exactly the same, they can be used to provide hands-on experience with sampling. By using a collection of tiles in a bag, children can investigate how repeated sampling, with replacement, can be used to predict the contents of the bag. Since the tiles are square, they can also be used to represent entries in a bar graph drawn on 1-inch grid paper. For example, class opinion polls can be quickly conducted by having each child place a tile in the column on a graph which corresponds to his or her choice.

To stimulate algebraic thinking, number sentences can be introduced in which each number is covered with tiles. The challenge for children is to figure out what is under each tile. Children will learn that sometimes they can be sure of the number covered, as in $4 + \boxed{} = 6$, while at other times they cannot, as in $\boxed{} + \boxed{} = 6$. This use of tiles lays the groundwork for introducing a variable.

ASSESSING CHILDREN'S UNDERSTANDING

Color Tiles are wonderful tools for assessing children's mathematical thinking. Watching children work with their Color Tiles gives you a sense of how they approach a mathematical problem. Their thinking can be "seen," in so far as that thinking is expressed through the way they construct, recognize, and continue spatial patterns. When a class breaks up into small working groups, you are able to circulate, listen, and raise questions, all the while focusing on how individuals are thinking. Here is a perfect opportunity for authentic assessment.

Having children describe their designs and share their strategies and thinking with the whole class gives you another opportunity for observational assessment. Furthermore, you may want to gather children's recorded work or invite them to choose pieces to add to their math portfolios.

> I learned that areas that are the same have all diffent perimiters. And that they are all diffent.

From: *Making Shapes*

> It is not posible to make a 3 by 4 rectangle and have 3/5ths red. I found this out by finding that it cant be done unless it's area is divisible by the number 5.

From: *Building Rectangles*

Models of teachers assessing children's understanding can be found in Cuisenaire's series of videotapes listed below.

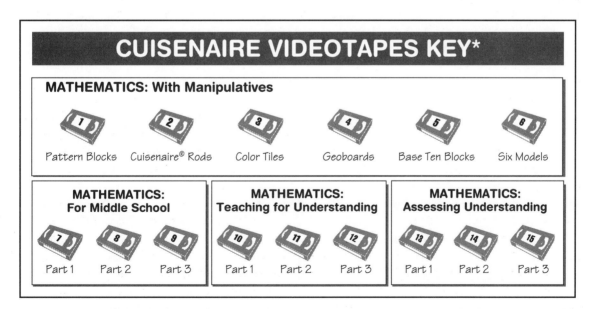

CUISENAIRE VIDEOTAPES KEY*

MATHEMATICS: With Manipulatives

1 Pattern Blocks	2 Cuisenaire® Rods	3 Color Tiles	4 Geoboards	5 Base Ten Blocks	6 Six Models

MATHEMATICS: For Middle School			**MATHEMATICS: Teaching for Understanding**			**MATHEMATICS: Assessing Understanding**		
7 Part 1	8 Part 2	9 Part 3	10 Part 1	11 Part 2	12 Part 3	13 Part 1	14 Part 2	15 Part 3

*See *Overview of the Lessons*, pages 16-17, for specific lesson/video correlation.

STRANDS

	PROBLEM SOLVING	COMMUNICATION	REASONING	CONNECTIONS	Geometry	Logic	Measurement	Number	Patterns/Functions	Probability/Statistics
A LOGIC PUZZLE	◆	◆	◆	◆	◆	◆			◆	
BORDER TILES	◆	◆	◆	◆	◆			◆		
BUILDING RECTANGLES	◆	◆	◆	◆	◆			◆		
HEXOMINOES	◆	◆	◆	◆	◆					
HOW DOES YOUR GARDEN GROW?	◆	◆	◆				◆			
HOW MANY ARRANGEMENTS?	◆	◆	◆						◆	◆
LISA'S DOG PEN	◆	◆	◆	◆	◆			◆		
MAKING FLAGS	◆	◆	◆					◆		
MAKING SHAPES	◆	◆	◆	◆	◆		◆			
PATTERNS AND FUNCTIONS	◆	◆	◆	◆				◆	◆	
SMALL SQUARE TABLES	◆	◆	◆	◆	◆				◆	
SQUARES OF FOUR	◆	◆	◆	◆	◆	◆		◆	◆	
SQUARES WITHIN SQUARES	◆	◆	◆	◆	◆			◆	◆	
SYMMETRY ALL AROUND	◆	◆	◆	◆	◆					
THE S-SHAPED FIGURE	◆	◆	◆	◆			◆			
TWO-THIRDS BLUE	◆	◆	◆	◆				◆		◆
WHAT HAPPENS TO THE AREA?	◆	◆	◆	◆	◆	◆	◆		◆	
WHAT'S YOUR PREDICTION?	◆	◆	◆	◆		◆				◆

Correlate
the Super Source™
to your curriculum.

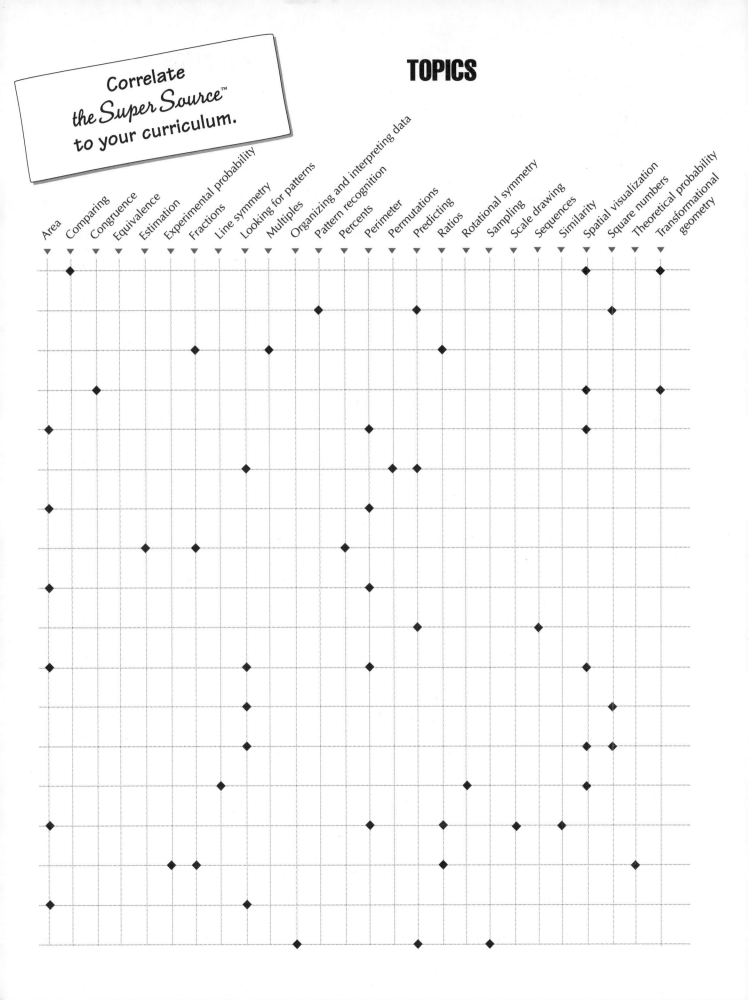

Area, Comparing, Congruence, Equivalence, Estimation, Experimental probability, Fractions, Line symmetry, Looking for patterns, Multiples, Organizing and interpreting data, Pattern recognition, Percents, Perimeter, Permutations, Predicting, Ratios, Rotational symmetry, Sampling, Scale drawing, Sequences, Similarity, Spatial visualization, Square numbers, Theoretical probability, Transformational geometry

Classroom-tested activities contained in these *Super Source*™ Color Tiles books focus on the math strands in the charts below.

...the *Super Source*™ **Color Tiles, Grades K-2**

Geometry	Logic	Measurement
Number	Patterns/Functions	Probability/Statistics

...the *Super Source*™ **Color Tiles, Grades 3-4**

Geometry	Logic	Measurement
Number	Patterns/Functions	Probability/Statistics

More SUPER SOURCE™ at a glance:
ADDITIONAL MANIPULATIVES for Grades 5-6

Classroom-tested activities contained in these *Super Source*™ books focus on the math strands as indicated in these charts.

the Super Source™ Tangrams, Grades 5-6

Geometry	Logic	Measurement
Number	Patterns/Functions	Probability/Statistics

the Super Source™ Cuisenaire® Rods, Grades 5-6

Geometry	Logic	Measurement
Number	Patterns/Functions	Probability/Statistics

the Super Source™ Geoboards, Grades 5-6

Geometry	Logic	Measurement
Number	Patterns/Functions	Probability/Statistics

the Super Source™ Snap™ Cubes, Grades 5-6

Geometry	Logic	Measurement
Number	Patterns/Functions	Probability/Statistics

the Super Source™ Pattern Blocks, Grades 5-6

Geometry	Logic	Measurement
Number	Patterns/Functions	Probability/Statistics

Overview of the Lessons

 See video key, page 11.

©1996 Cuisenaire Company of America, Inc.

Color Tiles, Grades 5-6

See video key, page 11.

A LOGIC PUZZLE

- Comparing
- Transformational geometry
- Spatial visualization

Getting Ready

What You'll Need

Color Tiles, 5 of each color per pair

Construction paper (red, yellow, blue, green—4 sheets of each)

5 x 5 Color Tile grid paper, 2 sheets per pair, page 90

Crayons (optional)

Overhead Color Tile and/or 5x5 Color Tile grid paper transparency (optional)

Overview

Children use Color Tiles and blank spaces to form a square according to a given set of rules. In this activity, children have the opportunity to:

- ◆ use logical reasoning
- ◆ develop designs that satisfy specific conditions
- ◆ discover alternative solutions

The Activity

You may want to post the rule so that children can refer to it as they determine their formation.

Introducing

- ◆ Distribute the construction paper, one sheet to each of sixteen children.
- ◆ Explain that children must display their papers as they determine a square seating arrangement—four rows of four—according to the colors of their papers. They must follow this rule:

    No child may sit next to, in front of, or behind a child with the same color.

- ◆ Allow the rest of the class to observe and comment as the group of sixteen makes the formation.
- ◆ If any children with the same colors are "touching," allow time for the group to discuss how to correct this.
- ◆ Have the observers record the final formation on grid paper.
- ◆ Ask children to identify color patterns in the formation.
- ◆ Collect the construction paper, then redistribute it to other children, challenging them to form a square seating arrangement with a different color pattern.

On Their Own

> ## Can you form 5-by-5 Color Tile squares according to a set of rules?
>
> - With your partner, use 20 Color Tiles—5 of each color—to form a square on a 5-by-5 grid. Your square will also have 5 blank spaces.
> - Make your square according to these rules:
>   - Tiles of the same color may not touch either up and down or across.
>   - Blank spaces may not touch either up and down or across.
>   - Tiles of the same color may not touch diagonally.
>   - Blank spaces may not touch diagonally.
>   - The order of the colors may not be the same in any 2 rows.
> - Record your square.
> - Now, make another 5-by-5 square, following the same rules. Do this either by changing your first square or by starting over again. Record this square.
> - Look for color patterns in your squares.
> - Be ready to talk about what you did.

The Bigger Picture

Thinking and Sharing

Ask pairs to check their squares to be sure they meet all the conditions. Then have volunteers post some of their squares.

Use prompts like these to promote class discussion:

- What strategies did you use to form your squares?
- Where did you run into problems?
- What patterns do you see?

Writing

Have children write a letter of advice to someone who is about to begin this activity. Suggest that they include an explanation of why their advice will be helpful.

Extending the Activity

Have children suggest ways to change the rules and/or change the number of tiles to make it harder to make the square.

Where's the Mathematics?

Children may initially apply a trial-and-error approach to this puzzle. Later, they may use transformational geometry by flipping certain arrangements to bring them into compliance with the rules. They may also find that an arrangement that does not work might do so if they rotated it and flipped some of its parts.

This activity presents a good opportunity for children to practice the math vocabulary that they will use in later studies of arrays: *row, column, horizontal, vertical,* and *diagonal.*

Children see early on that it is a good idea to place one tile of each color and one blank in each row. Once they have determined this, they may adopt the strategy of building one row at a time. For example, if the first row is red, green, blue, yellow, blank, the four choices for the second row are as shown.

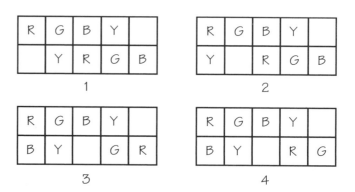

Each of the four scenarios above could lead to a number of solutions. Focusing on scenario 1, there would appear to be four choices for the third row. However, since one of those choices—red, green, yellow, blue, blank—would match the order of the tiles in the first row, there are only three choices for the third row.

R	G	B	Y	
	Y	R	G	B
R	G	B		Y

5

R	G	B	Y	
	Y	R	G	B
B	G		Y	R

6

R	G	B	Y	
	Y	R	G	B
G	B		Y	R

7

Focusing on scenario 5 (a continuation of 1), there are three possibilities for the fourth row; but one of them—blank, yellow, red, green, blue—is a match of the second row. Hence, there are two choices for the fourth row.

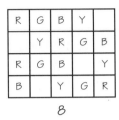

R	G	B	Y	
	Y	R	G	B
R	G	B		Y
B		Y	G	R

8

R	G	B	Y	
	Y	R	G	B
R	G	B		Y
B		Y	R	G

9

Finally, focusing on scenario 8 (the continuation of scenarios 1 and 5), there are three choices for finishing the puzzle.

R	G	B	Y	
	Y	R	G	B
R	G	B		Y
B		Y	G	R
G	R	B		Y

R	G	B	Y	
	Y	R	G	B
R	G	B		Y
B		Y	G	R
Y	G	R		B

R	G	B	Y	
	Y	R	G	B
R	G	B		Y
B		Y	G	R
Y	G	R	B	

Once children have found a solution, many may start again from scratch to find another. Some, however, may use the solution they found to find others. For example, flipping the first solution below over a vertical line gives the second, and flipping the second solution over a horizontal line gives the third.

R	G	B	Y	
	Y	R	G	B
R	G	B		Y
B		Y	G	R
G	R	B		Y

	Y	B	G	R
B	G	R	Y	
Y		B	G	R
R	G	Y		B
Y		B	R	G

Y		B	R	G
R	G	Y		B
Y		B	G	R
B	G	R	Y	
	Y	B	G	R

Rotating a solution so that the columns become rows may also yield new solutions.

In trying to find patterns among different solutions, children may note that even though every row may have one of each color and a blank, the columns may have as many as three of the same color or three blanks.

BORDER TILES

- Pattern recognition
- Square numbers
- Predicting

Getting Ready

What You'll Need

Color Tiles, about 20 each of
2 different colors per pair

Color Tile grid paper, page 91

Crayons

Overhead Color Tiles and/or Color
Tile grid paper transparency (optional)

Overview

Children use Color Tiles to model a series of squares and then figure out the number of border tiles and interior tiles in each square. In this activity, children have the opportunity to:

- ◆ identify and continue patterns
- ◆ explore square numbers
- ◆ make generalizations

The Activity

Introducing

- ◆ Discuss the concept of a *border*. Invite children to talk about where they have noticed borders.
- ◆ Ask children to use Color Tiles to make a square with a border of one color and inside tiles of a different color.
- ◆ Have children display or describe their squares.

On Their Own

> **What number patterns can you find by making Color Tile squares with borders?**
>
> - Working with a partner, use Color Tiles to make a 3-by-3 square. Use 1 color for the inside tile and a different color for the border tiles.
>
> - Build 3 more squares with your Color Tiles, each 1 tile longer and wider than the previous square. Again, use different colors for the border and for the inside.
>
> - Record each of your squares. Also record the number of tiles inside the square, the number of tiles in the border, and the total number of tiles used to make the square.
>
> - Look for patterns in your data. See if you can predict the number of inside tiles and the number of border tiles that you would need to build a 7-by-7 square and an 8-by-8 square. See if you can find a rule that can be used to find the number of inside tiles and border tiles for any size square.

The Bigger Picture

Thinking and Sharing

Have children help you create a class chart displaying the data for the four squares they built.

Use prompts like these to promote class discussion:

- How many border tiles and inside tiles did you use in your smallest square? How many in each of your next squares?

- Did you find any interesting relationships between the numbers? If so, what were they?

- What strategies did you use to find the number of inside and border tiles needed for the larger squares?

- Did you discover a rule for finding the number of inside and border tiles needed for any size square? If so, how? What is your rule?

Writing

Have children describe how they moved from building squares to making a rule.

Extending the Activity

Have children repeat the activity, making rectangles instead of squares. Tell some groups to start with a 3-by-6 rectangle and increase both the width and the length by one tile for each subsequent rectangle in the sequence. Tell other groups of children to begin with a 3-by-6 rectangle and increase the width by one tile and the length by two tiles for each subsequent rectangle in the sequence. Have children record their findings, look for patterns, and compare their results.

Where's the Mathematics?

The squares children build in this activity should produce the following data:

Dimensions	Number of inside tiles	Number of border tiles	Total number of tiles
3 by 3	1	8	9
4 by 4	4	12	16
5 by 5	9	16	25
6 by 6	16	20	36

Children may discover a number of patterns in the data. Some may notice that as the squares grow larger, the differences between the numbers of inside tiles are 3, 5, and 7, odd numbers increasing by two. Others may note that the numbers of inside tiles (1, 4, 9, and 16) are square numbers. They may decide that this is so because the inside tiles form a small square inside the larger one. In either case, children may continue their patterns to arrive at the number of inside tiles in a 7-by-7 square (25) and an 8-by-8 square (36).

Either of these patterns may start children thinking about a rule for the number of inside tiles. Children may notice that the inside tiles form a smaller square—a square whose sides are two tiles smaller than the original square. For example, the inside tiles of a 5-by-5 square form a 3-by-3 square. Many children may know that the product of these dimensions tells how many tiles are in the square. They may, therefore, generalize that to find the number of inside tiles needed to build a square of a certain size, they should subtract 2 from the number of tiles on a side and multiply that number by itself.

Some children may be able to represent this generalization algebraically, stating that the number of inside tiles in an S-by-S square is $(S - 2) \times (S - 2)$.

Children may also find patterns in the numbers of border tiles. For example, the number of tiles in the border of each successive square increases by 4.

Children may continue this pattern of adding 4 to determine the number of border tiles needed for successively larger squares. There will be 24 tiles in the border of a 7-by-7 square and 28 tiles in that of an 8-by-8 square.

Other children may use their square models to figure out the relationship between the number of tiles on a side of the square and the number of tiles in the border. They may generalize this relationship in different ways. They may say, for example, that the number of tiles needed in a border is four times the number of tiles on a side of the square minus 4 because the four corners are counted twice. Still other children may add the lengths of two of the sides of the original square and then add on the lengths of the other two sides, subtracting 2 from each of the second two sides first (the two corners having already been counted in the first two sides). Some might find the total number of border tiles by squaring the length of a side and then subtracting the number of tiles in the inner square.

Some children may try to represent these generalizations algebraically. Depending on the relationship they see, they might express the number of the tiles in the border of an S-by-S square as $(4 \times S) - 4$, or $S + S + (S - 2) + (S - 2)$, or $S^2 - (S - 2)^2$.

Children who have experience with number patterns may recognize a relationship between the number of tiles needed and the number of the square in the sequence of squares. For example, children may notice that the first square has 1 x 1 inside tiles; the second, 2 x 2 inside tiles; the third, 3 x 3 inside tiles, and so on. To find the number of tiles needed for a 7-by-7 square, these children may think: "This would be the fifth square in the sequence; therefore it would have 5 x 5, or 25, inside tiles. Subtracting this number from the total number of tiles in the square (7 x 7) tells me there would be 49 – 25, or 24, border tiles."

1st square
1 (1 x 1) inside tile

2nd square
4 (2 x 2) inside tiles

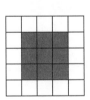

3rd square
9 (3 x 3) inside tiles

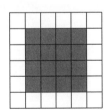

4th square
16 (4 x 4) inside tiles

BUILDING RECTANGLES

- **Fractions**
- **Multiples**
- **Ratios**
- **Equivalence**

Getting Ready

What You'll Need

Color Tiles, about 30, at least half of which are red, per pair

Color Tile grid paper, page 91

Crayons

Overhead Color Tiles and/or Color Tile grid paper transparency (optional)

Overview

Children use Color Tiles to build rectangles in which a specified fractional part is red. In this activity, children have the opportunity to:

- ◆ discover that a fraction has meaning only in terms of the whole of which it is a part
- ◆ find different ways to represent the same fractional part
- ◆ recognize multiples, equivalence, and ratios

Juan's Rectangle

Total number of tiles = 16
Number of blue tiles = 8

The Activity

Introducing

- ◆ Ask children to use their Color Tiles to create a rectangle of any size that is one-half blue.
- ◆ Call on two volunteers, one at a time, to display their rectangles and to explain why they think the blue tiles represent one half.
- ◆ See if everyone agrees. If not, allow discussion time for children to hear one another's arguments and to come to agreement.
- ◆ Invite suggestions for more ways of checking whether different rectangles are one-half blue.

26 the Super Source™ ◆ Color Tiles ◆ Grades 5-6   ©1996 Cuisenaire Company of America, Inc.

On Their Own

How can you use Color Tiles to show fractional parts of different rectangles?

- Working with a partner, use Color Tiles to build 2 different-sized rectangles to represent each of these situations:

    - 5/6 of the tiles are red

    - 2/3 of the tiles are red

    - 2/8 of the tiles are red

    - 3/5 of the tiles are red

- Record your solutions. For each rectangle, write both the total number of tiles and the number of tiles that are red.

- Be ready to talk about how you know your solutions are correct.

The Bigger Picture

Thinking and Sharing

Across the chalkboard, write the column headings *5/6 red, 2/3 red, 2/8 red,* and *3/5 red.* Have one pair of children post their solutions for each situation. Then ask other pairs, one at a time, to post any different solutions they may have.

Use prompts such as these to promote class discussion:

- How did you go about deciding how many tiles should be in each rectangle?

- How did you figure out how many red tiles to use?

- How did you find a second solution for each situation?

- How do the numbers in the fraction relate to the different tiles you used to create your rectangles?

- Look at the posted solutions. Are there any that you think are not correct? If so, tell why.

- Do you think that there are other solutions beyond those posted? Explain.

- How is it possible that there could be more than one solution for each situation?

Writing

Have children explain whether or not it is possible to create a 3-by-4 Color Tile rectangle that is 3/5 red. Encourage children to use Color Tiles to investigate this problem before writing their response.

Extending the Activity

1. Ask children to build rectangles in which each fractional part is specified. For instance, you might suggest that they try to build a rectangle that is 1/4 red, 3/8 blue, and 3/8 yellow.

Teacher Talk

Where's the Mathematics?

In this activity, children use proportional reasoning and a geometric setting to create their own models of fractional representations. As they build rectangles and test to see whether their rectangles fit the given conditions, children have an opportunity to enhance their understanding of what is meant by a fractional part of a whole.

Since the directions do not specify the size of the rectangles or the number of Color Tiles to use, children will need to experiment to make these determinations for themselves. Some children may begin by making a rectangle of a seemingly random size, and then adjusting the number of red tiles in the rectangle to try to produce the desired relationship. This may lead them to see that this is not always possible, and that the number of tiles used to build the rectangle determines whether or not the fractional part can be represented. For example, in building rectangles in which five sixths of the tiles are red, children may first build a 2-by-3 rectangle using five red tiles and one blue tile. They may then build a 2-by-4 rectangle and try to figure out how many of the eight tiles should be red so that five sixths are red. Once children discover that this is not possible using whole tiles, they may realize that the number of tiles they must use for their rectangles must somehow be related to the given fraction.

Some children may use their knowledge of equivalent fractions to make additional models. For example, to build rectangles that are two-thirds red, children may first create fractions equivalent to 2/3, such as 4/6 and 6/9, and then see if rectangles can be formed using the number of tiles indicated by the denominator. If so, they may realize that the numerator is the number of red tiles that should be used.

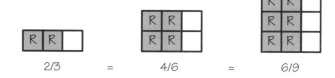

Other children may realize that for a rectangle to be, for example, three-fifths red, in every group of five tiles used, three must be red. These children may form groups of five tiles, three in each being red, and try to build their rectangles using one or more groups. In this way, they are sure to keep the ratio of red tiles to the total number of tiles constant.

When trying to build a second rectangle for a given situation, some children may think that if they add one red and one non-red tile to the set of tiles

2. Have children list situations drawn from their everyday experience that can be expressed as fractions (for example, in a class of 30 children, 16 are boys). Children could then select two or three of these situations and find different ways to model the relationships using Color Tiles.

used to form the first rectangle, they will keep the colors in the right proportion. For example, if children have used eight tiles to build a rectangle that is two-eighths red (two red, six non-red), they may try to build a second solution by increasing the number of red tiles to three and the number of non-red tiles to seven. This will enable them to build a ten-tile rectangle; however, when they test to see what fractional part is represented by red, they will find it to be three tenths and not two eighths. In considering why this strategy does not work, children may remember that amounts must be multiplied by the same factor (not increased by the same addend) to keep them in proportion. They may then try to apply this concept to obtain additional solutions.

Children with limited exposure to fractional representations may have trouble seeing how there could be more than one solution for each situation. They may say, for example, that in order for a rectangle to be five-sixths red, there must be six tiles, five of which must be red. These children may need help to understand that the fraction $\frac{5}{6}$ does not dictate that the whole must be six units; the whole may be any size. The fraction does indicate, however, that the ratio of red tiles to the total number of tiles is five to six, no matter how many tiles represent the whole.

In examining the class results and comparing the different solutions, some children may notice that the ratios of red tiles to total tiles for the models within each part of the activity produce equivalent fractions. These equivalences may become even more evident when listed sequentially, as is done below.

$$\frac{5}{6} = \frac{10}{12} = \frac{15}{18} = \frac{20}{24} = \frac{25}{30} = \ldots$$

$$\frac{2}{3} = \frac{4}{6} = \frac{6}{9} = \frac{8}{12} = \frac{10}{15} = \ldots$$

$$\frac{2}{8} = \frac{4}{16} = \frac{6}{24} = \frac{8}{32} = \frac{10}{40} = \ldots$$

$$\frac{3}{5} = \frac{6}{10} = \frac{9}{15} = \frac{12}{20} = \frac{15}{25} = \ldots$$

This list may help children to see that there are infinitely many solutions possible for each situation. Some may also notice that since $\frac{1}{4}$ is equivalent to the fractions in the third row, a rectangle consisting of four tiles, one of which is red, would be a solution for the third situation. As children recognize the connection between the models and the lists of fractions, they can better visualize and understand the concepts of equivalent fractions, fractional parts of a whole, and equal ratios.

HEXOMINOES

- Spatial visualization
- Congruence
- Transformational geometry

Getting Ready

What You'll Need

Color Tiles, 30 of 1 color per pair

Color Tile grid paper, page 91

Crayons

Envelopes for storing hexominoes

Overhead Color Tiles and/or Color Tile grid paper transparency (optional)

Overview

Children manipulate six Color Tiles in order to discover all the possible arrangements, or *hexominoes,* that can be made. In this activity, children have the opportunity to:

- ◆ devise strategies for finding shapes
- ◆ slide, flip, and turn shapes to check for congruence

The Activity

Introducing

- ◆ Label and display each of these figures using Color Tiles:

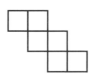 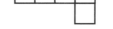 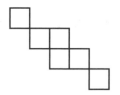

This is a hexomino.   This is a hexomino.   This is *not* a hexomino.

- ◆ Ask how all the figures are alike.
- ◆ Ask how the hexominoes differ from the figure that is not a hexomino.
- ◆ Try to elicit the ideas that
  - • a hexomino is a figure made up of six squares; and
  - • that at least one complete side of each of the squares touches another square along a complete side.

Point out that if one hexomino can be flipped and/or turned to match another hexomino exactly, the shapes are congruent and therefore are not different hexominoes.

On Their Own

Can you find all the different hexominoes using Color Tiles?

- Working with a partner, use Color Tiles of 1 color to make hexominoes. A hexomino is a shape made from 6 squares.

- At least 1 complete side of each of the tiles in a hexomino must touch 1 complete side of another tile.

Okay   Not okay

- Record each hexomino.

- When you think you have found all the hexominoes, cut them out.

- Check to make sure that each hexomino is different from all the others.

- Number your hexominoes and put them in an envelope. Write your names and the number of hexominoes on the envelope.

- Exchange envelopes with another pair. Check to see if any of their hexominoes are duplicates of each other. Mark any 2 that you think are exactly the same.

- Return the envelopes. Check your envelope to see if any duplicates were found.

- Decide on a way you can sort your hexominoes.

The Bigger Picture

Thinking and Sharing

Invite one or two pairs to post their hexominoes. Ask children to point out any duplicates, missing hexominoes, or figures that are not hexominoes.

Use prompts like these to promote class discussion:

- Do you think that you have found all the possible hexominoes? Why or why not?

- In what ways do the hexominoes differ from one another?

- Did you use a strategy to find new shapes? If so, describe what you did.

- Did you find any patterns while making your hexominoes? Did you use these patterns when sorting them? If so, how?

- Did sorting your hexominoes help you find others that were missing? If so, explain.

Extending the Activity

1. Have children examine their hexominoes and predict which of them could be folded along the lines to form a covered box (a cube). Have children then cut out those hexominoes and fold them to check their predictions.

Where's the Mathematics?

Children will use many different strategies to search for all possible hexominoes. Although most children will begin by searching in a seemingly random fashion, some may proceed with a more organized approach. For example, children may begin by placing five tiles in a row, adding on the sixth tile in a variety of different locations to form different hexominoes. They may then work with four tiles in a row, adding on two extra tiles in different locations. Other children may begin with a 2-by-3 rectangle, moving one tile at a time out of the rectangle to form different shapes. No matter what strategies they use, children will discover that there are many different shapes that can be formed with six tiles. Thirty-five hexominoes are shown below.

It should not be expected that all children will find all the different hexominoes. However, each pair of children should find a significant number of hexominoes and be able to eliminate duplicates from their collection.

©1996 Cuisenaire Company of America, Inc.

2. Encourage children to investigate the perimeters of their hexominoes. Have them sort their hexominoes according to perimeter and discuss their findings.

Some children may decide to make all the hexominoes they can and check for duplicates when they think they have made every possible hexomino. Others may check for duplication as they build new hexominoes. In testing for congruence by flipping and turning their cutout shapes, children learn to recognize how shapes that appear to be different may actually be congruent. For example, although at first glance, children may think that the following two shapes are different hexominoes, one is actually a flip and a rotation of the other.

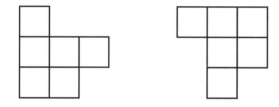

Children will have different ways of sorting their shapes. Some may sort according to the greatest number of tiles that appear in a row. Others may sort their shapes based on letters of the alphabet that they resemble. In sorting their shapes, children may discover duplicates that they had not seen before. They may also discover new hexominoes.

It is important that children share their strategies for finding, checking, and sorting their hexominoes. This helps them to understand that problems can be solved in many different ways and that different people may take different approaches to solving the same problem. Furthermore, by sharing strategies, children learn about a variety of problem-solving strategies they can use to solve problems in the future.

HOW DOES YOUR GARDEN GROW?

- Area
- Perimeter
- Spatial visualization

Getting Ready

What You'll Need

Color Tiles, about 25 per child

Color Tile grid paper, page 91

18-Tile Garden Plot outline,
1 per child, page 93

Overhead Color Tiles and/or Color
Tile grid paper transparency (optional)

Overview

Children use Color Tiles to solve a problem involving area and perimeter. In this activity, children have the opportunity to:

- ◆ reinforce the concepts of area and perimeter
- ◆ examine the relationship between area and perimeter
- ◆ develop critical and logical thinking skills
- ◆ use modeling to solve a problem

The Activity

Some children may need to be reminded that area is the space inside a shape and that perimeter is the distance around a shape. Be sure to show children that they can find the area of a design by counting the Color Tiles inside it and the perimeter by counting the sides of the tiles along its outer edge.

Introducing

- ◆ Display this design and ask children to think of it as a model for a garden plot.

- ◆ Have children copy the design with Color Tiles.

- ◆ Ask children how they would find both the area and the perimeter of this garden plot. Have them determine these values and share their results.

- ◆ Point out that if a garden this shape were enclosed by a fence, the length of the fence would be the same as the garden's perimeter.

On Their Own

Bobby, Sarah, and Juan bought just enough fencing to fit exactly around their garden. Now, they want more space for planting. Which idea for enclosing more space will work?

- Use 18 Color Tiles to construct the garden plot.

- With your group, experiment with the garden plot by moving or adding tiles to see which of these ideas will work:

    1. Buy more fencing.
    2. Use the same amount of fencing, but use it in a different way.
    3. Use even less fencing.

- Record your models. Record the area and perimeter on each model. Then cut out your recordings.

- Be ready to explain what you discovered about each idea for expanding the garden.

Bobby, Sarah, and Juan's garden plot

The Bigger Picture

Thinking and Sharing

Invite children to discuss their general responses to the activity. Then label three columns: *Idea 1, Idea 2,* and *Idea 3,* and have children post their drawings to show how the three ideas in the problem could work.

Use prompts like these to promote class discussion:

- What do you think of the first idea? Give reasons for your answer.
- How did you make the second idea work?
- How was it possible to get even more space with less fencing?
- Looking at the shapes that represent the second and third ideas, what do you notice?
- Were you surprised to find that all three ideas would work? If so, tell why.

Writing

Ask children to describe how they changed the garden to represent each idea and how those changes affected the area and perimeter of the garden.

Extending the Activity

1. Have children design a sequence of gardens, all with the same area. Ask them to arrange them from the one that would require the least amount of fencing to surround it to the one that would require the most.

Where's the Mathematics?

In this activity, children explore area and its relationship to perimeter by attempting to solve a problem three different ways. Their explorations with the tiles may help them to see that changes to shapes may have differing effects on area and on perimeter. This recognition may spark children to pursue their investigation of each of the three ideas, even if they were originally skeptical about one or more of them.

The original garden:

Area = 18
Perimeter = 22

As children begin their investigation, they discover that in order to add more space to the garden, they must add tiles to their model. They can then find many different ways to show that the first idea will work. In each of the models shown below, both the area and the perimeter are greater than those of the original garden.

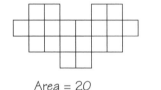

Area = 20
Perimeter = 26

Area = 21
Perimeter = 24

Groups that conclude that only the first idea will work should be encouraged to continue investigating with the tiles.

Proving that the second idea will work may take some more doing. Many children may believe that if the area increases, the perimeter will increase as well. In fact, their initial attempts to build models with greater areas may confirm their suspicions. Either by chance or by further investigation, children may realize that by arranging the tiles in particular ways, they can add new tiles without adding units of fencing to their garden. Two examples of these kinds of arrangements are shown below.

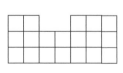

Area = 19
Perimeter = 22

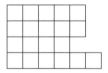

Area = 20
Perimeter = 22

2. Challenge children to create an original garden for which not all of the three children's suggestions could work.

The third idea of increasing the area of the garden while decreasing the amount of fencing may seem illogical or impossible to many children. However, in their work on the other two ideas, children may have discovered that not all tiles in their models contribute units of perimeter; only those on the borders do. With this in mind, children may try to build models that have more interior tiles (tiles all of whose sides touch other tiles) and fewer border tiles. These interior tiles contribute to the area without contributing to the perimeter. Some examples are shown below.

Area = 20
Perimeter = 18

Area = 25
Perimeter = 20

Many children will be surprised to find that all three ideas will work. They may also be surprised at the number of different solutions generated by the class. Activities such as this one help children to see that there are often different ways to solve problems producing varying, but effective, solutions.

HOW MANY ARRANGEMENTS?

PROBABILITY/STATISTICS • PATTERNS/FUNCTIONS

- **Permutations**
- **Looking for patterns**
- **Predicting**

Getting Ready

What You'll Need

Color Tiles, 12 of each color per pair

Color Tile grid paper, page 91

4- and 5-Tile Arrangements, several sheets per pair, pages 94-95

Crayons

Overview

Children use Color Tiles to arrange a given number of colors in as many different ways as possible. In this activity, children have the opportunity to:

- ◆ work informally with permutations and factorials
- ◆ discover patterns in data
- ◆ use patterns to make predictions

The Activity

It is important to emphasize that in each arrangement, each of the three letters must appear only once. This means that ADD and NAN are not acceptable arrangements of the letters NAD.

Introducing

- ◆ Write three different letters on the chalkboard.
- ◆ Challenge children to put them in order in as many different ways as they can.
- ◆ Then, as children describe different arrangements, write them down until all possible arrangements have been listed. There should be six different arrangements. (For example, the letters NAD can be arranged *NAD, NDA, ADN, AND, DAN,* and *DNA.*)
- ◆ Explain that in mathematics, the different ways of arranging items are called *permutations.*

On Their Own

Can you figure out how many ways there are to arrange different-colored tiles in different orders?

- Work with a partner. Place Color Tiles in a line to find all the possible ways to arrange colors in different orders. Do this for 1 color, 2 colors, 3 colors, 4 colors, and 5 colors.

- For each number of colors you investigate, choose only the appropriate number of tiles from the 4 Color Tile colors. For example, if you are looking for arrangements of 3 colors, make lines of 3 Color Tiles of different colors. To find arrangements of 5 colors, use a stack of 2 tiles (such as green/blue) to represent the 5th color.

- Find ways to record your solutions. Make sure you don't record the same arrangement twice.

- Look for a pattern that you could use to predict the number of possible arrangements of 10 colors, 20 colors, or even more colors.

The Bigger Picture

Thinking and Sharing

Have volunteers show the solutions for one through four colors. If other children disagree, let them explain their thinking. Then invite children to discuss the five-color arrangements. Children who made lists or tree diagrams to find all the arrangements can show their work. Those who used logical reasoning to solve the problem can explain their thinking. Finally, compile the results in a chart, indicating the number of colors and the number of different arrangements.

Use prompts like these to promote class discussion:

- How many arrangements are possible with one color? two colors? three? four? five?

- How did you make sure that you had found all the possible arrangements of the colors?

- How did you make sure as you worked that you were not repeating any arrangement?

- How did you determine the number of arrangements that were possible for ten, twenty, or any number of colors?

- Do you see any patterns in your results? If so, describe them.

Extending the Activity

Have children find the number of nonlinear arrangements that can be made using a given number of tiles. For example, have them investigate to find the number of different squares that can be made using four different-colored tiles.

Where's the Mathematics?

It is likely that children will use different strategies for finding the different ways to arrange the colors. Some may search randomly, whereas others may use a more organized approach. Children will discover that there is one possibility for one color, two possibilities for two colors, and six possibilities for three colors. A tree diagram showing the six possibilities for three colors is shown below.

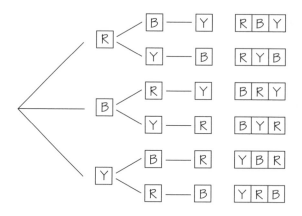

As the number of colors increases, children are likely to discover that they need some kind of strategy in order to avoid repeating arrangements. One possible approach involves starting with one color, pairing it with another, and finding all combinations that start with those two colors. The first color is then paired with a different color and, again, combinations starting with those two colors are formed. The chart below shows the results of using this strategy to find four-color arrangements.

R	B	Y	G
RB YG	BR YG	YR BG	GR BY
RB GY	BR GY	YR GB	GR YB
RY BG	BY RG	YB RG	GB RY
RY GB	BY GR	YB GR	GB YR
RG BY	BG RY	YG BR	GY RB
RG YB	BG YR	YG RB	GY BR

For five colors, listing all the arrangements is tedious. Logical reasoning can make this task easier. For example, some children might reason that since a fifth color added to a four-color arrangement could appear in any one of five positions, each of the 24 different four-color arrangements could produce five different five-color arrangements. Thus, the number of different five-color arrangements would be 5 x 24, or 120. Other children may reason that if they can figure out the number of arrangements that begin with one particular color, they can multiply that number by 5 (since there are five different colors that arrangements could begin with) to figure out the total number possible. For example, in the table on the next page, red is paired with each possible second color (forming the columns), a third color is selected, and possible arrangements of the fourth and fifth colors are made. F is used to represent the fifth color.

RB	RY	RG	RF
RB Y GF	RY B GF	RG B YF	RF B GY
RB Y FG	RY B FG	RG B FY	RF B YG
RB G YF	RY G BF	RG Y BF	RF Y GB
RB G FY	RY G FB	RG Y FB	RF Y BG
RB F YG	RY F BG	RG F BY	RF G BY
RB F GY	RY F GB	RG F YB	RF G YB

Since beginning with red yields 24 arrangements, and there are five possible colors to begin with, the total number of possibilities is 5 x 24, or 120.

Number of Colors	Number of Arrangements
1	1
2	2
3	6
4	24
5	120

Once they have found a solution for five colors, children may look at their data and search for a pattern. Children may notice that the numbers of arrangements form a pattern in that each successive number is obtained by multiplying the previous number by the number of colors in the next larger-sized arrangement. For example, the number of arrangements possible using four colors is four times the number of arrangements possible using three colors, and the number possible using five colors is five times the number possible using four colors. The fact that these multipliers increase by one each time may lead children to discover that in each case, the number of arrangements is the product of all the numbers from 1 through the number of colors. For example, the number of arrangements of three colors is 1 x 2 x 3, or 6. The number of arrangements of four colors is 1 x 2 x 3 x 4, or 24. Recognition of this pattern will allow children to calculate the number of arrangements that could be made with any number of colors.

You may want to take this opportunity to introduce the term factorial and its symbol "!" Explain that the mathematical expression 5! means 5 x 4 x 3 x 2 x 1.

The patterns children find in their results are based on the Basic Counting Principle, a concept that children will encounter later in their study of permutations and combinations. Although it is not necessary to explore these concepts further at this point, exposure to the ideas of factorial and permutations, and the meaning and use of these terms, can provide a good basis for subsequent study.

LISA'S DOG PEN

Getting Ready

What You'll Need

Color Tiles, about 150 per pair

Color Tile grid paper, page 91

Overhead Color Tiles and/or Color Tile grid paper transparency (optional)

Overview

Children use Color Tiles to determine how to create a shape with a given perimeter and the greatest possible area. In this activity, children have the opportunity to:

◆ build scale models with dimensions that result in a specified perimeter

◆ discover that shapes with the same perimeter may have different areas

◆ reinforce the idea that squares are rectangles

◆ deepen their understanding of the formula for finding the area of a rectangle

Perimeter = 22 inches
Area = 24 square inches

The Activity

Introducing

◆ Review the fact that Color Tiles have sides that are 1-inch long.

◆ Display a rectangle made with Color Tiles and ask children to tell how long and how wide it is. Establish that these measurements are called the dimensions of the rectangle.

◆ Have children determine the perimeter of the rectangle and explain how they got that measurement.

◆ Do the same for the area of the rectangle.

On Their Own

> Lisa plans to use 48 feet of fencing to enclose the rectangular dog pen she is going to build. Can you help Lisa to give her dog the largest pen possible?
>
> - Working with your partner, use Color Tiles to build models of possible dog pens. Let each Color Tile represent 1 square foot.
>
> - Make several different model rectangles, each with a perimeter of 48 feet.
>
> - Record your models and their dimensions.
>
> - Figure out which rectangle Lisa should use to obtain the greatest area for her dog pen.
>
> - Copy the rectangle you chose on another sheet of paper and label its length, width, and area.
>
> - Be ready to discuss your work.

The Bigger Picture

Thinking and Sharing

Begin by asking children the dimensions of the rectangle they made that has the largest area. Post the various rectangles and invite comparisons.

Use prompts such as these to promote class discussion:

- How did you go about finding rectangles with perimeters of 48 feet?

- How did you find the areas of the rectangles you made?

- Can a 12-by-12-foot square be the solution to this problem? Why or why not?

- What are the dimensions of the pen with the greatest possible area?

- How do you know that this is the largest pen that can be enclosed by 48 feet of fencing?

- Based on the models you made, what generalizations can you make about the areas of rectangles that have the same perimeter?

Extending the Activity

1. Repeat the activity with the following addition: Lisa remembers at the last moment that she has not allowed for a gate so that her dog can get in and out of the pen. She buys a 2-foot-wide gate. What is the largest possible rectangular dog pen that Lisa can now build?

2. Repeat the activity, removing the restriction that the pen must be rectangular. Encourage children to look for alternative shapes that would be suitable for a dog pen.

Where's the Mathematics?

Some children may begin by making a 1-by-48 rectangle, thinking its perimeter will be 48 units. When they discover that its perimeter is actually 98 units (and that its area is 48 square units), they should realize the error in their thinking.

Children may build models for some or all of the rectangles that have a perimeter of 48 units. Some may do this in a random way. Others may create a series of models like the following:

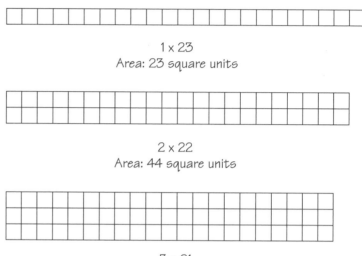

1 x 23
Area: 23 square units

2 x 22
Area: 44 square units

3 x 21
Area: 63 square units

Some children may begin by building a series of models like those shown above and then decide to skip some when they notice that the closer the two dimensions get to each other, the greater the area becomes.

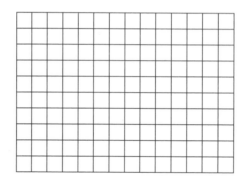

10 x 14
Area: 140 square units

Children may be surprised to find that there could be so many different rectangles with the same perimeter. They may also be surprised to discover how much the areas of these rectangles vary. Once children realize this, they may want to organize their search in some way that enables them to consider all possible models. Some children may record the dimensions of the rectangles they find in a table and look for patterns that might be helpful.

Length (feet)	Width (feet)	Area (square feet)
23	1	23
22	2	44
21	3	63
20	4	80
19	5	95
18	6	108

Examining the data, children may notice that by decreasing the length of a rectangle by 1 unit and increasing the width by 1 unit, they can create another rectangle that has a perimeter of 48 units. For children who find area by counting tiles, the table may also help them to see that the area of a rectangle can be calculated by multiplying its length by its width.

Some children may say that Lisa's dog pen should be an 11-by-13-foot rectangle with an area of 143 square feet. Others may say that it should be 12 feet by 12 feet, with an area of 144 square feet. Some children may argue that if it were 12 feet by 12 feet, it would be a square and not a rectangle. This can be an opportunity to reinforce the idea that a square is a special kind of rectangle. It may help if children list the essential elements of a rectangle and those of a square side by side and compare the lists.

RECTANGLE	SQUARE
Polygon	Polygon
Quadrilateral	Quadrilateral
Four right angles	Four right angles
Opposite sides congruent and parallel	Opposite sides congruent and parallel
	All four sides congruent

Use the lists to help children see that all squares are rectangles because they fit all the descriptions under "rectangle," but not all rectangles are squares because not all rectangles fit the last description under "square."

MAKING FLAGS

Getting Ready

What You'll Need

Color Tiles, at least 100 per pair

Color Tile grid paper, page 91

Crayons

Overhead Color Tiles and/or Color Tile grid paper transparency (optional)

Overview

Children use Color Tiles to design flags. They then identify the part of each flag represented by each color both as a fraction and as a percent. In this activity, children have the opportunity to:

◆ determine fractional parts of a whole

◆ change fractions to equivalent percents

◆ estimate percents

◆ understand that a fractional part or a percent is determined by the whole of which it is part

The Activity

Introducing

B	B	G	G
B	G	G	G
B	R	R	R
B	B	B	B

◆ Display the following "flag" made with 16 Color Tiles. Ask children to figure out what fractional part of the flag is blue.

◆ After they have agreed that 8/16, or 1/2, of the flag is blue, ask children what percent of the flag is blue. Elicit the idea that the flag is 50 percent blue because 1/2 is equivalent to 50 percent.

◆ Have children explain why the flag is 5/16 green.

◆ Invite volunteers to estimate what percent of the flag is green, and have children explain their thinking.

On Their Own

Can you figure out the fractional part and percent that each color represents in a Color Tile flag?

- Use Color Tiles to make rectangular designs for flags.

- Make your flags different sizes and patterns. Use as many colors as you like in each flag.

- Record your flags.

- For each flag, work with your group to figure out the fractional part represented by each color. Record these numbers.

- Now estimate the percent represented by each color in each flag. Record these numbers.

- Be ready to explain how you found your fractions and percents.

The Bigger Picture

Thinking and Sharing

Give all groups an opportunity to display their flag designs and to give their fractions and percents as well as their reasoning. If class members disagree with the values, have children work together to come to agreement.

Use prompts such as these to promote class discussion:

- What fractional part and percent of the whole is each color in your flag?

- What was the easiest part of this activity? What was the most difficult?

- What was your group's strategy for determining the fractions? for estimating the percents?

- What do you notice about the sum of your percents? What does this tell you about your estimates?

Writing

Have children choose one of their flag designs to describe. Have them give the fractions and percents that represent the different colors and explain how they determined these.

Extending the Activity

Have children repeat the activity using Pattern Blocks instead of Color Tiles, thus allowing children to produce a wider variety of different-shaped flags with more intricate designs.

Where's the Mathematics?

Children will most likely begin this activity by making flags that have pleasing designs. They may make these designs without giving too much thought to the task of figuring out the fractional parts and percents represented by the different colors. Once they start trying to figure out these values, children may decide to alter their designs to make their calculations easier. They may change the number of tiles used to make the flag or change the number of tiles of a particular color. Some children may even decide to use exactly 100 tiles to make their flags, making the percents easy to figure out.

R	R	R	R	R	R	R	R	R	R
R	G	G	G	G	G	G	G	G	R
R	G	Y	Y	Y	Y	Y	Y	G	R
R	G	Y	B	B	B	B	Y	G	R
R	G	Y	B	R	R	B	Y	G	R
R	G	Y	B	R	R	B	Y	G	R
R	G	Y	B	B	B	B	Y	G	R
R	G	Y	Y	Y	Y	Y	Y	G	R
R	G	G	G	G	G	G	G	G	R
R	R	R	R	R	R	R	R	R	R

$^{40}/_{100}$ red – 40%
$^{28}/_{100}$ green – 28%
$^{20}/_{100}$ yellow – 20%
$^{12}/_{100}$ blue – 12%

G	G	G	G	G	G	G	G	G	Y	Y	B	B	B	B	B	B	B	B	B
G	G	G	G	G	G	G	G	G	Y	Y	B	B	B	B	B	B	B	B	B
Y	Y	Y	Y	Y	Y	Y	Y	Y	Y	Y	Y	Y	Y	Y	Y	Y	Y	Y	Y
B	B	B	B	B	B	B	B	B	Y	Y	G	G	G	G	G	G	G	G	G
B	B	B	B	B	B	B	B	B	Y	Y	G	G	G	G	G	G	G	G	G

$^{28}/_{100}$ yellow – 28%
$^{36}/_{100}$ green – 36%
$^{36}/_{100}$ blue – 36%

Some children may first select the colors they want to use in their flag and then carefully figure out how many of each color they should use so that the fractions and percents will be easy to figure out. They may then use this select group of tiles to make their flag. Others may focus more on the design of the flag, keeping an eye on the proportions of colors being used.

R	R	R	B	B	B	Y	Y	Y
R	R	R	B	B	B	Y	Y	Y
R	R	R	B	B	B	Y	Y	Y
R	R	R	B	B	B	G	G	G
R	R	R	B	B	B	G	G	G
R	R	R	B	B	B	G	G	G

⅓ red – a bit more than 33%
⅓ blue – a bit more than 33%
⅙ yellow – a bit more than 16%
⅙ green – a bit more than 16%

To figure out the fractional part of their flags represented by each color, most children will count the number of tiles of each color used and use these numbers as numerators of fractions in which the denominator is the total number of tiles used in the flag. Some children may decide to reduce these fractions, and others may not. Depending on the fraction and the children's familiarity with percents and their equivalents, it may or may not be beneficial to reduce the fraction before estimating the percent. For example, if children find that their flag made from 30 tiles is 6/30 blue, then reducing 6/30 to 1/5 may help them to recognize that the flag is 20 percent blue. However, if their flag is made from 50 tiles, 34 of which are blue, it may be easier for children to think that 34 out of 50 is equivalent to 68 out of 100, or 68 percent.

Many children will have had some informal experience with common percents like 50, 25, and 75. Some children may think of 1/3 as 33 percent and 2/3 as 66 percent, reasoning that 3/3 is 100 percent, so 1/3 of 100 must be about 33, and 2/3 of 100 must be about 66. When children obtain a fraction that does not translate easily, they may think of a fraction close to theirs for which they do know an equivalent. For example, if children have a flag design in which 5/16 of the tiles are red, they might reason that 5/16 is close to 4/16, or 1/4, and therefore they would estimate that the flag is a little more than 25 percent red.

To calculate their percents, children may also think in terms of the percent represented by each tile. For example, in a flag made from 50 tiles, each tile represents 2 percent of the total flag (since $100 \div 50 = 2$). Children can then multiply the number of tiles of any one color by 2 percent to find out the percentage of the flag represented by that color. This kind of thinking will also work well for estimating percents. For example, if a flag is made up of 48 tiles or 55 tiles, each tile is slightly more or slightly less than 2 percent of the flag, and percents can be adjusted accordingly.

Children should find that the sum of their percents is very close to 100 percent. If this is not the case, children should recognize this as an indication that their estimates may not be accurate enough.

As children compare their work with the work done by other groups, they can see that the fractional parts and percents represented by certain colors depend on the size of the whole flag. For example, two different flags may contain 10 red tiles; however, those 10 red tiles represent 1/4, or 25 percent, of a flag made from 40 tiles, and only 1/10, or 10 percent, of a flag made form 100 tiles. This is an important mathematical concept for children to understand and to be able to apply in their work with fractions and percents.

MAKING SHAPES

Getting Ready

What You'll Need

Color Tiles, about 50 per pair

Color Tile grid paper, page 91

Overhead Color Tiles and/or Color Tile grid paper transparency (optional)

Overview

Children use Color Tiles to create a variety of shapes that have the same area. They then find and compare the perimeters of the shapes they made. In this activity, children have the opportunity to:

- ◆ strengthen their understanding of the concepts of area and perimeter
- ◆ discover that shapes with the same area do not necessarily have the same perimeter
- ◆ recognize how the compactness of a shape affects its perimeter

The Activity

Introducing

- ◆ Show children this shape made with Color Tiles.

- ◆ Ask them to tell what is meant by the area and the perimeter of the shape.
- ◆ Establish that the *area* is the number of square units inside the shape and that the *perimeter* is the length, or distance, around the shape.
- ◆ Call on a few children to find the shape's area and perimeter. Then invite children's comments about the two measurements.

On Their Own

What can you predict about the perimeters of different shapes that have the same area?

- Working with a partner, make 10 different Color Tile shapes, each with an area of 22 square units. Your shapes must follow this rule:

  At least 1 complete side of every Color Tile must touch at least 1 complete side of another Color Tile.

- Record each shape on grid paper. You may have to tape some sheets together to record some of the larger shapes. Find and label each shape's perimeter.

- Discuss your results with your partner. Be ready to talk about what you notice.

The Bigger Picture

Thinking and Sharing

Have children share their results and talk about what they discovered about the perimeters of their shapes. Then call for the shape with the shortest perimeter. When that has been determined, post that shape on the left side of the chalkboard. Let children continue posting different shapes, ranging from the shortest to the longest perimeter.

Use prompts such as these to promote class discussion:

- What did you notice about area and perimeter?

- How can you explain the differences in perimeters of the shapes with the same area?

- How would you describe the shapes with shorter perimeters? with longer perimeters?

- Did you always count the edges of the border tiles in a shape to find its perimeter, or did you find shortcuts? Explain.

Writing

Ask children to write about some of the things they know about shapes that have the same area.

Extending the Activity

1. Have children study the shapes that were posted during the activity. Ask them to try to create and record other shapes with areas of 22 square units and with perimeters that were not represented. Then call children together to share their work and to show that no shape with an area of 22 square units has a perimeter longer or shorter than those already found.

Teacher Talk

Where's the Mathematics?

Children often confuse the concepts of area and perimeter. In the process of finding perimeters of shapes with a given area, children may more clearly define each concept for themselves and create their own strategies for remembering the difference.

Many children assume that if one shape has a certain area and perimeter, then all shapes with that area will have the same perimeter. In this activity, children discover that shapes can have the same area but different perimeters. The perimeters of the 22-tile shapes made according to the rules range from 20 to 46 units.

Children can observe that shapes with longer perimeters are often more spread out than those with shorter perimeters, which tend to be more compact. Some children may see that in the shapes with shorter perimeters, the tiles share more sides with each other; therefore, fewer sides are left exposed on the outside, or perimeter, of the shape. For example, in this compact shape, each square is labeled with the number of exposed sides that contribute to the perimeter. Five of the squares are completely enclosed, so they do not contribute to the perimeter.

2	1	1	1	1	1	2	
1	0	0	0	0	0	1	
2	1	1	1	1	1	1	3

Area = 22
Perimeter = 22

In this elongated shape, every square has at least two sides that are exposed and contribute to the perimeter.

3	2	2	2	2	2	2	2	2	2	2	2	2	2	2	2	2	2	2	2	2	3

Area = 22
Perimeter = 46

2. Have children create and record as many different shapes as they can that have a perimeter of 22 units. Tell them to arrange the shapes according to area, from least to greatest. Challenge children to prove that they have made the shapes with the least and greatest areas having this perimeter.

Children may notice that the perimeters are all even numbers. This happens because the net result of moving a tile is always an even number of exposed sides. In the example below, a tile is moved from the end of the top row and replaced at the end of the bottom row. When the tile is removed, 2 units of perimeter go with it. However, the tiles to the left of and below the removed tile each have one more side exposed, so the perimeter remains the same. When the tile is replaced at the end of the third row, the third tile in that row has one more side covered up, but the replaced tile has three exposed sides, giving the perimeter a net gain of 2.

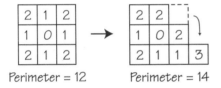

Perimeter = 12   Perimeter = 14

Another way to explain why all perimeters have even numbers of units is by tracing a shape's perimeter completely with a pencil. To get back to the starting point, the pencil has to move 1 unit to the left for every unit it moved to the right, and it must move one unit up for every unit it moved down.

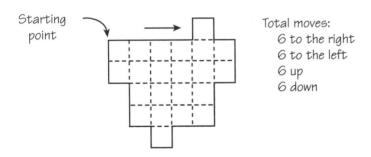

Starting point

Total moves:
  6 to the right
  6 to the left
  6 up
  6 down

Because of this, the total left-right moves must always be multiples of two, and the total up-down moves must also be multiples of two.

PATTERNS AND FUNCTIONS

* Sequences
* Predicting
* Patterns

Getting Ready

What You'll Need

Color Tiles, at least 40 blue and 22 red per pair

Overhead Color Tiles and/or Color Tile grid paper transparency (optional)

Overview

Children figure out how to determine the number of Color Tiles needed for designs in a sequence without actually creating the designs. In this activity, children have the opportunity to:

◆ look for patterns in both numbers and designs

◆ collect and organize data

◆ use patterns to make predictions

Design #	Red Tiles	Blue Tiles	Total
1	2	2	4
2	2	3	5
3	2	4	6

The Activity

Introducing

◆ Display the following sequence of Color Tiles.

| R | B | B | R |

| R | B | B | B | R |

| R | B | B | B | B | R |

◆ Have children make the next two designs in the sequence with their Color Tiles.

◆ Ask children how many tiles of each color it takes to create each of these new designs.

◆ Call on volunteers to explain how they decided what the two new designs should be.

On Their Own

When you know how a sequence of designs begins, can you figure out how many tiles of each color will be needed to build any design in that sequence?

- Look at the following sequence of designs:

- Predict how many Color Tiles you would need for the 10th design in this sequence without building all 10 designs. Here's how.

  - Create several more designs in the sequence.

  - Record the number of tiles of each color and the total number of tiles in each design.

  - Look for patterns in your data.

  - Continue to create designs in the sequence until you can use your findings to describe, in detail, the 10th design in the sequence without building it.

- Be ready to talk about how you made your prediction.

The Bigger Picture

Thinking and Sharing

Invite children to share their solutions and their reasoning. Then have them help you create a class chart with these column headings: *Design Number, Red Tiles, Blue Tiles, Total.*

Use prompts like these to promote class discussion:

- Did you notice any patterns in your designs? If so, describe them.

- What patterns did you find in your data?

- What did you do to find the number of tiles of each color in the tenth design in the sequence?

- How can you use the numbers in the first column of the chart to determine the numbers in the other columns?

- How would you use your data to predict the fifteenth design? the hundredth design?

Extending the Activity

Have pairs use Color Tiles to build the first three or four designs in a sequence of their own creation. They can then exchange their designs and try to predict the number of tiles of each color and the total number of tiles that will be needed to build the tenth, fifteenth, and hundredth designs in each other's sequences.

Where's the Mathematics?

On a purely visual level, children will note that the designs have two reds at each end, square groups of four blue tiles in the middle, and single red tiles separating the blue groups. They may see that for each new design in the sequence, a blue group is added and a red tile is added to separate it from the other blue groups.

By studying their actual designs and the patterns in their data, children may be able to make connections among the design number, the numbers of red and blue tiles, and the total number of tiles in the design. Here is a chart showing the data for the first ten designs:

Design Number	Red Tiles	Blue Tiles	Total
1	4	4	8
2	5	8	13
3	6	12	18
4	7	16	23
5	8	20	28
6	9	24	33
7	10	28	38
8	11	32	43
9	12	36	48
10	13	40	53

In looking at the data within columns, children can observe that the numbers in the *Red Tiles* column increase by 1 and that the numbers in the *Blue Tiles* column increase by 4; they may even say that the numbers of blue tiles are a set of multiples of 4. In the *Total* column, children may note that the numbers have an even-odd pattern, that the units digits alternate between 8 and 3, and that the numbers increase by 5. By continuing the patterns they find within the columns, children may be able to determine the data for the fifteenth design (red tiles: 18; blue tiles: 60; total tiles: 78). It would be tedious, though, to find the data for the hundredth design in this way. It is by looking for patterns across the columns that children can discover a way to make predictions about the hundredth design.

In looking at the data across columns, most children will recognize that the numbers in the *Red Tiles* column are three more than the numbers in the *Design Number* column. They should also see that the numbers in the *Blue*

Tiles column are four times the numbers in the *Design Number* column. With this information, children can determine that the hundredth design has 100 + 3, or 103 red tiles; 100 x 4, or 400 blue tiles; and 103 + 400, or 503 tiles in all.

Children who are more experienced at finding patterns might enjoy the challenge of finding a pattern that connects the numbers in the *Design Number* column with those in the *Total* column. One way to do this is through addition:

Design Number	Add		Total
1	7	=	8
2	11	=	13
3	15	=	18
4	19	=	23

Each number added is four times the design number plus three. So the tenth design has 10 + (4 x 10) + 3, or 53 tiles, and the fifteenth has 15 + (4 x 15) + 3, or 78 tiles.

A less complicated but harder-to-discover pattern is to multiply the design number by 5 and then add 3.

Design Number		Total
1	1(5) + 3	8
2	2(5) + 3	13
3	3(5) + 3	18
15	15(5) + 3	78
100	100(5) + 3	503

For children who are ready, this activity provides a springboard for writing algebraic expressions. If the design number is represented by the variable n, the number of red tiles is $n + 3$, the number of blue tiles is $4n$, and the total number of tiles is $5n + 3$.

SMALL SQUARE TABLES

GEOMETRY • PATTERNS/FUNCTIONS

- Area
- Perimeter
- Looking for patterns
- Spatial visualization

Getting Ready

What You'll Need

Color Tiles, at least 40 per pair

Color Tile grid paper, page 91

Overhead Color Tiles and/or Color Tile grid paper transparency (optional)

Overview

Children use Color Tiles to model a problem involving the number of tables needed to seat different numbers of party guests. In this activity, children have the opportunity to:

- investigate perimeter
- generalize a formula about perimeter
- use modeling to solve a problem

The Activity

Some children may think the perimeter would be 8 units (2 x 4 units). Others may think it would be 7 units (incorrectly subtracting 1 from 8, based on the observation that the squares share one side). Help them to see the errors in their thinking.

Introducing

- Review the concept of *perimeter.*
- Display one Color Tile and have children determine that its perimeter is 4 units (or 4 inches).
- Next, ask children to think about what the perimeter of a rectangle would be if it were made from two Color Tiles.
- Have children use their Color Tiles to verify that the perimeter would be 6 units (or 6 inches).

On Their Own

Suppose you are having a party and you want to put small square tables together to make a larger rectangular table. What is the smallest number of tables you need to seat 12 friends?

- Working with a partner, use as few Color Tiles as necessary to model a rectangular table that will seat 12 friends.
  - At least 1 complete edge of each tile must touch 1 complete edge of another tile.
  - Only 1 person can sit at the edge of each small table.
- Use grid paper to record your best arrangement.
- Now repeat this procedure as you model a table that will seat 16 friends.
- Find the smallest number of square tables you would need to seat 20, 50, 100, and 99 friends.
- See if you can figure out a way to determine how many tables you would need for any number of friends. Draw pictures that help to explain your thinking.

The Bigger Picture

Thinking and Sharing

Invite pairs to share their results for tables that will seat 12 friends, 16 friends, 20 friends, 50 friends, 100 friends, and 99 friends. Then ask if any pairs discovered a rule that could be used to determine the number of tables needed for any given number of friends. Have these pairs present their rules and explain their thinking.

Use prompts such as the following to promote class discussion:

- What was the smallest number of tables needed to seat 12 friends?
- What was the smallest number of tables needed to seat 16 friends? 20 friends? 50? 100?
- Why did you arrange the tables as you did?
- Did you try any other arrangements? If so, what did you notice?
- How did you determine the smallest number of tables needed to seat 99 friends?
- Did anyone find a rule that works for any number of friends? If so, what is the rule and how does it work? Does it also work for odd numbers of friends? Explain.

Extending the Activity

Tell children to imagine that a hostess wants to have three separate rectangular tables for herself and her 63 guests. Challenge children to find the best shape to make each of the tables so that the smallest number of square tables is needed.

Where's the Mathematics?

In modeling tables to seat 12 people, children learn that several rectangles are possible and that the fewest tiles are in the rectangle that consists of a single line of Color Tiles.

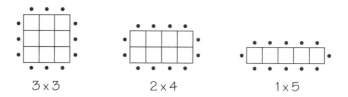

When they model the table for 16 friends, children may begin to suspect that the fewest tiles will always be in the rectangle with a single line of tiles.

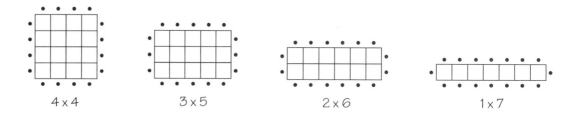

There are five possible rectangular tables that will seat 20 people, the 1-by-9 table requiring the fewest tiles. Instead of continuing to build models of the seating arrangements, some children will look at what they have already built and notice that if they subtract 2 (the sum of the places at the ends of the long tables) from the number of people to be seated and then divide the remaining number by 2 (the number of places along the length of the table) they will get the smallest number of tiles. For example, if the table seats 20, they can subtract 2 for the ends of the table and then divide by 2, or $(20 - 2) \div 2 = 9$.

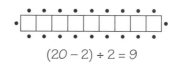

$$(20 - 2) \div 2 = 9$$

The same reasoning shows that the minimum number of tiles needed to model a table of 50 people is $(50 - 2) \div 2$, or 24.

Instead of continuing to use tiles to model the tables, children may begin to look for patterns in their data.

Number of people	Number of tiles
12	5
16	7
20	9

Looking at the data, there is a pattern of odd numbers in the second column. Children may want to fill in the "holes" in their data by seeing what the results would be for 14 and 18 people. As it turns out, 14 people would sit at a table represented by 6 tiles and 18 would sit at a table represented by 8 tiles. Therefore, the number of people has an even-number pattern, and the number of tiles has a consecutive number pattern. Using these patterns, children could count up by twos for the number of people and by ones for the number of tiles to find the smallest number of tiles. This would be tedious, though, for a table of 50, and it would be easy to make errors.

If children look across the columns in the data, they may be able to come up with a way to connect the number of people to the number of tiles. The table for 12 is modeled with 5 tiles, which is 1 less than half of 12. Likewise, 7 is 1 less than half of 16, and 9 is 1 less than half of 20.

Children can verify this pattern by using known data. The number of tiles needed to model a table for 18 must be 1 less than half of 18—that is, $(18 \div 2) - 1$, or 8 tiles. Using the pattern for new data, children can determine that 50 people would require a table of $(50 \div 2) - 1$, or 24 tiles, and 100 people would require a table of $(100 \div 2) - 1$ or 49 tiles.

Children who are ready for algebra may be interested in using the following expression, based on the patterns above, to find the number of tiles. The variable n represents the number of people.

$$(n \div 2) - 1$$

After they begin to test the formula on various numbers, some children will probably ask what happens if there is an odd number of people to be seated. They may realize that this solution is appropriate only for even numbers of people because rectangles made up of square units all have even perimeters. Encourage children to look for a practical solution to the problem of seating an odd number of people. For example, the most practical way to seat 99 people might be to use 49 square tables and leave one place empty.

SQUARES OF FOUR

- Looking for patterns
- Square numbers

Getting Ready

What You'll Need

Color Tiles, about 70 per pair

Color Tile grid paper, page 91

Overhead Color Tiles and/or Color Tile grid paper transparency (optional)

Overview

Children investigate the different-sized squares that can be made using 2-by-2 Color Tile squares. In this activity, children have the opportunity to:

- ◆ use smaller shapes to create larger shapes
- ◆ organize information in a table
- ◆ identify patterns
- ◆ make generalizations

The Activity

Introducing

- ◆ Ask children to create squares of different sizes using Color Tiles.
- ◆ Call on volunteers to display different-sized squares and tell how many tiles it took to build each one.
- ◆ Point out that these squares can be referred to as *squares of four*, *squares of nine*, and so on.

On Their Own

What can you find out about Color Tile squares made from "squares of 4?"

- Working with a partner, investigate squares that are made up of "squares of 4". A "square of 4" looks like this:

- Start with a single Color Tile square. Record this square and label it *Square 1.*

- Now build the Color-Tile square that has 1 "square of 4." Record this square and label it *Square 2.*

- Build the next larger square made from squares of 4. Record and label this *Square 3.*

- Your first 3 squares should look like these.

- Continue building larger squares that contain squares of 4. Record and label each.

  square 1   square 2   square 3

- Make a table showing the number of each square in the sequence and the number of squares of 4 that can be found in each.

- Look for patterns in your table. How many squares of 4 would there be in the 10th square? the 50th square? the 100th square?

- Try to find out how to find the number of squares of 4 that could be found in any square in the sequence. Be ready to explain your thinking.

The Bigger Picture

Thinking and Sharing

Have children help you create a class chart showing the data for the different-sized squares. If some pairs found squares that other children did not, have them share their data. Include data for the tenth, fiftieth, and one-hundredth square in the table. Then ask if any pairs found a way to figure out the number of squares of four for any given square in the sequence. If so, have them explain their rule and give an example.

Use prompts like these to promote class discussion:

- What did you notice about squares made from squares of four?

- What patterns did you discover in your data?

- How did the patterns help you to find the solutions for the tenth, fiftieth, and one-hundredth squares?

- Were you able to find a rule that will help determine the number of squares of four in any square in the sequence? If so, what is that rule? How does it work?

Extending the Activity

1. Have children extend their charts to include a third column for recording the total number of tiles in each square. Have children record this information and compare it to the data in the other columns of the table. Ask them to look for patterns and to describe what they notice.

Where's the Mathematics?

If pairs of children are limited to 70 Color Tiles, they will be unable to build beyond the fifth square, which requires 64 tiles. Therefore, children must record their data so that patterns emerge. Children who record their data in a random fashion may find it more difficult to recognize patterns than those who create a table like the one below:

Squares in the sequence	Squares of 4
1	0
2	1
3	4
4	9
5	16

If children use a table like this one, they are likely to notice that the numbers in the second column are square numbers and that this sequence continues with 25, 36, 49, and so on. Some children may also discover another pattern in these numbers: The differences continually increase by 2 (the difference between 0 and 1 is 1, between 1 and 4 is 3, between 4 and 9 is 5, between 9 and 16 is 7, and so on). Using this pattern, children may say that the difference between 16 and the next number must be 9, so the next number is 16 + 9, or 25.

As children examine these tables, the patterns they discover can help them to name the number of squares of four in the tenth square. Applying these patterns to find the square of four in the fiftieth and hundredth squares, though, is tedious and can result in mathematical errors. To find the information about the fiftieth and hundredth squares (and any given square), children may try to formulate a rule. A rule allows them to figure out the number of squares of four in any square of the sequence without having to find the number for all the previous squares.

2. Have children repeat the activity using squares of nine. In constructing their tables, have children include a third column for recording the total number of tiles in each square. Ask them to compare their results to those obtained using squares of four.

Not all children will discover a rule. However, some may examine the table to determine how to go from a number in the left-hand column to the corresponding number in the right-hand column. They may notice that a number in the right-hand column is the square of the *previous* number in the left-hand column. To go from the left to the right, then, they multiply one less than the number on the left by itself to get the number on the right.

Squares in the sequence		Squares of 4
1	$(1 - 1) \times (1 - 1) = 0 \times 0$	0
2	$(2 - 1) \times (2 - 1) = 1 \times 1$	1
3	$(3 - 1) \times (3 - 1) = 2 \times 2$	4
4	$(4 - 1) \times (4 - 1) = 3 \times 3$	9
5	$(5 - 1) \times (5 - 1) = 4 \times 4$	16

Once children make this discovery, they probably will test this idea out on the squares listed in the table and find it to be true of all the known squares. Then they conclude that the fiftieth square has $(50 - 1) \times (50 - 1)$, or 2,401 squares of four, and that the one-hundredth square has $(100 - 1) \times (100 - 1)$, or 9,801 squares of four. Children who have experience in dealing with algebraic formulas may be able to state the rule with variables. For example, letting n stand for the number of the square in the series, the formula for the number of squares of four would be:

$$(n - 1)^2$$

SQUARES WITHIN SQUARES

- • Spatial visualization
- • Looking for patterns
- • Square numbers

Getting Ready

What You'll Need

Color Tiles, 100 per pair

Color Tile grid paper, page 91

Overhead Color Tiles and/or Color Tile grid paper transparency (optional)

Overview

Children use Color Tiles to build a 10-by-10 square and search for smaller squares within the larger square. In this activity, children have the opportunity to:

- ◆ develop counting techniques and recording systems
- ◆ use patterns to solve problems
- ◆ learn about square numbers

The Activity

Some children may need to be reminded that a right angle *is the angle formed by a square corner.*

Introducing

- ◆ Have children examine a Color Tile with a partner and talk about all the things they notice.
- ◆ Establish that a Color Tile is a square because all of its sides are congruent and all of its angles are right angles. Explain that a Color Tile is a 1-by-1 square because it is 1 unit long by 1 unit wide.
- ◆ Ask children how many squares it will take to build the next larger square. Then have partners build that square (a 2-by-2).
- ◆ Have children examine their 2-by-2 square and ask how many different squares they see in their figure. Elicit that there are five squares to be discovered, including the largest one.

On Their Own

> **How many squares can you find in a 10-by-10 Color Tile square?**
>
> - Working with a partner, use Color Tiles to build a 10-by-10 square.
>
> - Decide how to search for all the squares that are in your square.
>
> - Record the sizes of the squares you find and the number of squares of each size.
>
> - Look for patterns that might help you in your search.

The Bigger Picture

Thinking and Sharing

Invite partners to share their solutions and explain how they worked. Then have them help you create a class chart showing the dimensions of the squares and the number of squares of each size. Have children work together to resolve any discrepancies.

Use prompts such as these to promote class discussion:

- What strategy or strategies did you use to find as many squares as you could?

- Were some squares harder to find than others? If so, which ones and why?

- How did you keep track of the squares you found?

- Did you find any patterns that could help solve this problem without actually counting each square? If so, describe what you noticed.

- How did you decide you had counted all the squares?

- Do you see any patterns in the class chart? If so, describe them.

In recording the sizes of the squares, some groups may have used dimensions, such as 1-by-1 or 1 x 1, while others may have used the number of tiles in the square, such as 4 tiles, 9 tiles, and so on. You may want to include these different representations in the class chart.

Some children may recognize the different numbers of squares as perfect squares.

Writing

Have children explain how they might go about finding all the squares in a 20-by-20 Color Tile square.

Extending the Activity

1. Have children investigate to find the total number of squares contained in Color Tile squares of different sizes, from 1-by-1 squares to 10-by-10 squares. Suggest that they look for patterns that might help them to figure out the total number of squares contained in any size Color Tile square.

2. Ask children to use a calculator to find the smallest possible Color Tile square that contains 1,000 different squares.

Where's the Mathematics?

Visualizing overlapping squares is not an easy task. Children may find it helpful to use different-colored crayons to outline each square on grid paper.

To find all the squares in a 10-by-10 Color Tile square, children must realize that they need to look beyond the obvious. They may readily find the 1-by-1 squares, the 10-by-10 square, and some of the 2-by-2, 3-by-3, 4-by-4, and 5-by-5 squares. However, other squares may be more difficult to see, especially if they overlap squares that children have already identified. For example, in searching for 5-by-5 squares, children may identify the four squares shown in Figure A below. They may not as easily recognize many of the other 5-by-5 squares, some of which are shown in Figures B and C, since these overlap the squares in Figure A.

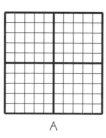
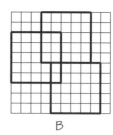
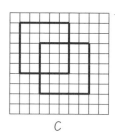

A   B   C

If children appear overwhelmed with the task because of the size of the square, you may want to suggest that they first look at a smaller square, such as a 3-by-3 or 4-by-4.

Once children recognize that there are many squares to be found, they may think to investigate the problem by looking at a similar, smaller problem. For example, children may investigate to find the number of squares in a 4-by-4 square. Here they will find 1-by-1 squares (the individual tiles), the 4-by-4 square, and the 2-by-2 and 3-by-3 squares shown below.

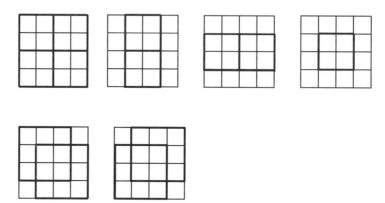

This may help children to find overlapping squares in the 10-by-10 square more easily. It may also help them develop a procedure for counting the squares. For example, to identify all of the 4-by-4 squares in their 10-by-10 square, children may start in the upper left-hand corner and move tile-by-tile through the square, counting 4-by-4 squares for which the tile they land on is the upper left-hand tile in a 4-by-4 square. The first few steps of this search method are shown on the next page.

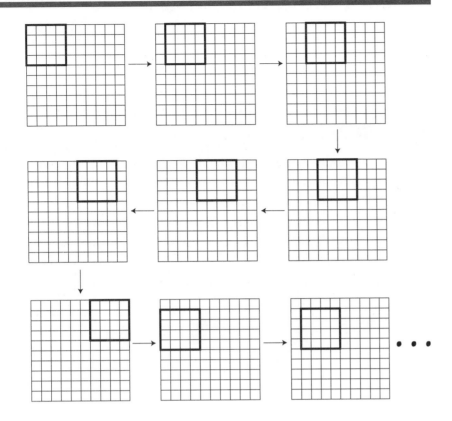

Some children may begin their search visually but then look for patterns in their data that may help them to predict how many squares of different sizes they can expect to find. If they have begun by counting larger squares first, their data may take the form of the chart shown at the right.

Size of Square	Number of Squares
10 x 10	1
9 x 9	4
8 x 8	9
.	.
.	.
.	.
1 x 1	100

Children may notice that the numbers in the second column of the chart are perfect squares. Some children may look at this data and hypothesize that the number of 7-by-7 squares might be 16 (the next largest perfect square). Once they check this and find it to be the case, children may feel they have identified the pattern and complete the chart using perfect squares.

Children who do not recognize the numbers as perfect squares may need to add the number of 7-by-7 squares (16) to the table before they see that the numbers in the second column increase by consecutive odd numbers (3, 5, 7, and so on). Recognition of this pattern may help these children anticipate the number of successively smaller squares that can be found in the 10-by-10 square.

When the data are assembled in the class chart, children may identify the patterns discussed above. They may also notice another pattern: The product of the dimensions of the largest square (a 10-by-10) is the number of the squares of the smallest size that can be found; the product of the dimensions of the second largest square (a 9-by-9) is the number of squares of the second smallest size (a 2-by-2) that can be found; and so on. It is important for children to see how the recognition of patterns such as these can help them to solve problems.

Size of Square	Number of Squares
10 x 10	1
9 x 9	4
8 x 8	9
7 x 7	16
6 x 6	25
5 x 5	36
4 x 4	49
3 x 3	64
2 x 2	81
1 x 1	100

SYMMETRY ALL AROUND

- Line symmetry
- Rotational symmetry
- Spatial visualization

Getting Ready

What You'll Need

Color Tiles, 20 of each color per pair
Color Tile grid paper, page 91
Crayons
Tracing paper
Mirrors (optional)

Overview

Children create Color Tile designs by repeatedly bordering a figure. They then look for symmetry in their designs. In this activity, children have the opportunity to:

- become familiar with line and rotational symmetry
- observe how designs formed by surrounding a core design retain the symmetry of the core design
- use spatial visualization skills

The Activity

Point out that some shapes, like this one, have many lines of symmetry; others may have only one line of symmetry or no symmetry at all.

Be sure children understand that the turn producing the exact match must be less than a full 360-degree turn.

Introducing

- Give children copies of the figure shown at the right.
- Ask children to try to draw a line of symmetry through the figure.
- Suggest that children check for line symmetry by folding their paper along the line they drew to see if both sides coincide.
- Invite a few children who found different lines of symmetry to stand together and hold up their work. Then have everyone draw all four lines of symmetry on their shape and mark its center with a big dot.
- Have children trace the shape on tracing paper.
- Now have children put the tracing carefully over the original figure, press a sharp object into the center of the dot, and give the tracing a one-quarter turn. Ask whether the two versions cover each other exactly.
- Explain that if a shape and a copy of it match exactly when one is placed over the other and turned, the shape is said to have *rotational symmetry.*

On Their Own

What can you discover about symmetry in a "growing" design?

- Work with a partner to "grow" a design by surrounding Color Tiles of 1 color with tiles of another color.

- First decide which colors you will call Color 1, Color 2, Color 3, and Color 4.

- Use 4 tiles of Color 1 to make a design. Each tile must touch at least 1 other tile along a complete edge.

- Record this design.

- Use Color 2 to put a border around your Color-1 design. Do this by placing 1 tile next to each outside edge of the Color-1 design.

- Make another border around Color 2 using Color-3 tiles, then another around Color 3 using Color-4 tiles.

- If you want to continue, and you have enough tiles, start again with Color 1 and keep making borders around each color.

- Record your final design. Then cut it out.

- Examine both your Color-1 design and your final design for lines of symmetry and rotational symmetry. A design has rotational symmetry if you can turn the design so that the turned version is an exact match of the original design.

- Repeat the activity, starting with a different Color-1 design.

- Be ready to talk about what you noticed each time you examined your designs.

The Bigger Picture

Thinking and Sharing

Have children post their designs and describe the kinds of symmetry they found.

Use prompts like these to promote class discussion:

- What did you notice about your designs as you "grew" them?

- How is the shape of your final design like the shape of your original design?

- Did anyone make more than three borders? If so, what did you notice?

- How did you test for line symmetry? for rotational symmetry?

- Did anyone start by making a design that had no lines of symmetry?

- Did anyone make a design that had many lines of symmetry?

- What did you notice about the symmetry in your original and final designs?

- Are the designs that have lines of symmetry symmetrical with respect to color as well as to shape? Explain.

Extending the Activity

1. Have children select one of the original designs they used in the activity. Have them repeat the bordering procedure, except this time each border should completely surround the figure inside it; that is, children should put a tile next to each edge and each corner of the design. After they

Where's the Mathematics?

In this activity, children use *iteration*—that is, a repeated procedure—to create a design from a core figure. When children compare their designs with those made by others, they will be able to notice the variety that results from using just four tiles. Here are the first three iterations for two different starting figures.

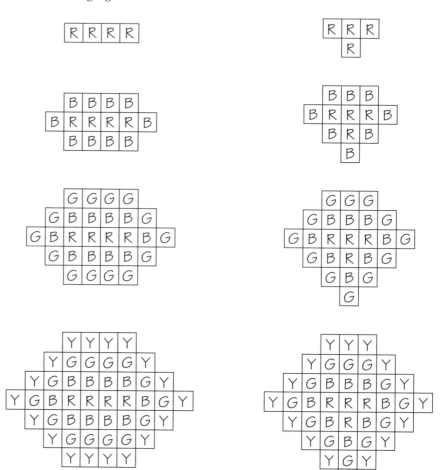

have made three borders, have children compare their results with the results of the original activity.

2. Have children repeat both the activity and the extension described above using more than four tiles in the original figure.

The way in which the designs develop may surprise children. The rectangular design made of four tiles in a row is growing toward a hexagonal shape. The T-shaped design is growing toward a square, or diamond, shape.

By experimenting, or by analyzing the designs of others, children discover that the types of symmetry in the starting design, if any, are retained in all the iterations. For example, the rectangular starting design on the previous page and each iteration have a vertical line of symmetry and—if children consider lines of symmetry going through the center of Color Tiles—a horizontal line of symmetry.

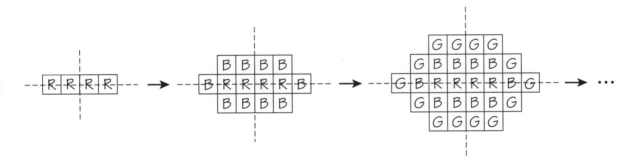

All of the iterations of the rectangle made from four tiles in a row have half-turn rotational symmetry; that is, they can be rotated 180 degrees (or a half turn) with the result that the rotated figure is an exact match of the original.

The T-shaped design does not have rotational symmetry, since it must be rotated a full 360-degree turn for the rotated figure to match the original design. If children consider lines of symmetry that go through the center of Color Tiles, the T-shape and its iterations do have a vertical line of symmetry.

THE S-SHAPED FIGURE

- Scale drawing
- Ratio
- Area
- Perimeter
- Similarity

Getting Ready

What You'll Need

Color Tiles, 150 per pair

Color Tile grid paper, page 91

Overhead Color Tiles and/or Color Tile grid paper transparency (optional)

Overview

Given a scale model of a shape made from Color Tiles and the area of the larger shape it represents, children figure out the scale used and the perimeter of the larger polygon. In this activity, children have the opportunity to:

- ◆ explore ratios used in scale drawings
- ◆ use ratios and proportions to solve a problem

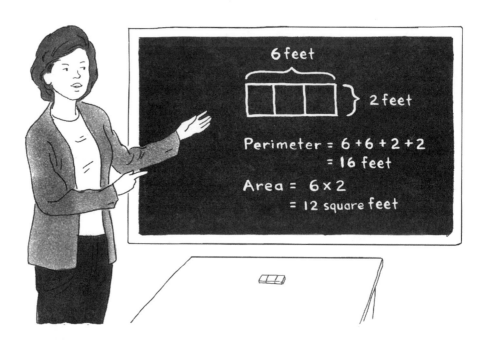

The Activity

If some children are having trouble understanding the concept of scale, *you can use Color Tiles to show them successive enlargements of a square. As the square grows, it grows equally on all sides. Enlargements or reductions are always* similar *to the original figure.*

Help children to understand that although the scale model is smaller than the rectangle it represents, its length and width are proportional to those of the larger rectangle, making the two rectangles similar.

Introducing

- ◆ Show children a rectangle made with three Color Tiles. Ask how to find the area and the perimeter of the rectangle.

- ◆ Now ask children to think of the longer side as six feet. Explain that this makes the rectangle a scale model of a much larger rectangle.

- ◆ Ask children what length is represented by the edge of each Color Tile in the scale model. Confirm that if the length of the rectangle is six feet, each edge represents two feet.

- ◆ To check children's understanding, have them find the area and perimeter of the larger rectangle that the scale model represents.

©1996 Cuisenaire Company of America, Inc.

On Their Own

Can you use Color-Tile models of a figure to help you find the perimeter of a larger version of the same figure?

- Work with a partner. Use Color Tiles to make this S-shaped figure. Then find its perimeter (in inches) and its area (in square inches).

- Consider this figure a scale model of a bigger S-shaped figure that has an area of 400 square inches. How can you find the perimeter of this larger figure?

  - Build larger models and look for patterns that will help you answer the question.

  - Remember that as your figures become larger, each Color Tile must grow into a larger square.

- Use both words and diagrams to tell how you arrived at your solution.

The Bigger Picture

Thinking and Sharing

Call on pairs, one by one, to share their solutions. Record each solution on the chalkboard. Then let children take turns explaining their procedures for finding their solution.

Use prompts such as these to promote class discussion:

- What is the perimeter of the larger S?
- How did you figure its perimeter?
- What length does the side of one tile in the model represent?
- How are the perimeters of the small S and the larger S related?
- How are the areas of the small S and the larger S related?
- Are there other ways this problem could be solved? Explain.

Extending the Activity

1. Have children use Color Tiles to create S-shaped figures with side-length ratios of 1:2, 1:3, and 1:4. Have them find the area and perimeter of each S, make a chart of their findings, and discuss their results.

2. Have children use Color Tiles to create a figure shaped like a letter other than S. Have them explore enlargements of their letter, recording data for side lengths, areas, and perimeters.

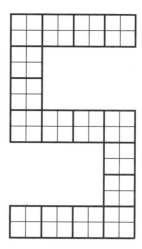

Teacher Talk

Where's the Mathematics?

As children consider the problem of finding the perimeter of the larger S, they may begin by doubling each length of the small S. To do this, they might replace each Color Tile with a square made from four Color Tiles as shown below.

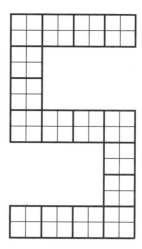

However, children may realize that the area of this S is only 64 square inches, not nearly as large as the 400 square inches of the large S-shape in the problem. Alternatively, some children might use numbers, reasoning that if each tile edge of the scale model were equal to 2 inches in the larger S, then the area of one tile would be 2 x 2, or 4. Since 16 tiles x 4 is only 64, it follows that a side of a tile must be worth more than 2 inches.

Another strategy children may use is to break down the problem into steps. They may realize that in order to find the perimeter of the larger S, they need to know how the side of a square in the small S relates to the side of a square in the larger S. They might begin to write down what they know about each S and look for ways to compare the information:

area of larger S = 400 square inches
area of small S = 16 square inches
ratio of areas = 400 to 16 = 400/16 = 25/1
The area of the larger S is 25 times the area of the small S.

Children who reach this point might jump to the conclusion that the perimeter and area relationships are the same—the perimeter of the larger S is 25 times that of the small S, or 25 x 34, or 850 inches. That is not the case. Children who do not reach this false conclusion might continue to reason along these lines:

The area of the larger S is 25 times the area of the small S.
So each tile in the small S represents 25 square inches in the larger S.
So the side of each tile in the small S stands for 5 inches of perimeter in the larger S.

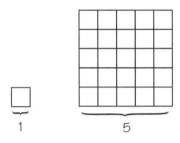

1 represents 5.

The perimeter of the small S is 34 inches.
The perimeter of the larger S is 34 times 5, or 170 inches.

Children may realize that they can use ratios to summarize and describe the relationships in side lengths, areas, and perimeters between the two figures:

ratio of areas = 400 to 16 = 25 to 1
ratio of side lengths = 5 to 1
ratio of perimeters = 170 to 34 = 5 to 1

After children have had the opportunity to compare and discuss their methods and results, they may be able to come up with a generalization: Side lengths and perimeter increase in the same ratio. In this problem, the scale is 5 to 1. The area increases with the square of the side length, so the ratio of the areas is 5^2 to 1^2, or 25 to 1.

TWO-THIRDS BLUE

- Fractions
- Ratios
- Experimental probability
- Theoretical probability

Getting Ready

What You'll Need

Color Tiles, about 100 per group

Small paper bags, 1 per group

Overview

Children use Color Tiles to represent a fractional part of a whole and to investigate probability. In this activity, children have the opportunity to:

- ◆ reinforce the understanding that the value of a fractional part is determined by the whole from which it comes
- ◆ gain experience with experimental probability
- ◆ collect and analyze data
- ◆ begin to realize the difference between mathematical probability and experimental probability

The Activity

Introducing

- ◆ Place four Color Tiles in a bag—two red, one blue, and one yellow.
- ◆ List the contents of the bag on the chalkboard.
- ◆ Ask children what fractional part of all the tiles in the bag are red tiles. Confirm that the answer is one half.
- ◆ Have children discuss whether, if you drew one tile from the bag without looking, you would be as likely to pick a blue or a yellow as a red tile.
- ◆ Establish that since one half of all the tiles are red, the theoretical probability of reaching into the bag and pulling out a red tile is one out of two, or one half.
- ◆ Tell children to imagine that they drew tiles from the bag, one at a time, replacing each after it was drawn. Ask children if they think that after ten or twenty draws, one half of the tiles they drew would be red.

Children should recognize that even though theoretically one half of the tiles drawn should be red, experimentally this may not be exactly what happens.

On Their Own

If you sample tiles from a bag of Color Tiles in which $\frac{2}{3}$ of the tiles are blue, should you expect that $\frac{2}{3}$ of the tiles you sample will be blue?

- Work with your group to assemble an assortment of Color Tiles that is $\frac{2}{3}$ blue.

- Put your tiles into a paper bag and write the names of the people in your group on the outside of the bag.

- Exchange bags with another group.

- Without looking, draw a tile from the bag, record its color, and return it to the bag. Shake the bag to mix the tiles for the next draw. Do this several times.

- Continue sampling tiles until you have enough data to be sure that the number of blue tiles either is or is not $\frac{2}{3}$ of the total number of tiles in the bag.

- Now open the bag and check its contents. Discuss how your data relates to the actual contents of the bag.

- Exchange bags with a different group and repeat the experiment.

- Be ready to talk about your results.

The Bigger Picture

Thinking and Sharing

Have children return their bags to the groups that filled them and discuss their findings with those groups.

Use prompts like these to promote class discussion:

- What are some examples of a set of tiles in which two thirds are blue?

- After you had drawn several tiles from the bag, did you expect any particular results? Explain your answer.

- How did your sampling experiments help you to know whether or not two thirds of the tiles in a bag were blue?

- Did you discover a relationship between the fractional part of the tiles in the bag that were blue and the fractional part of the total number of samples that were blue? How would you explain this?

- Might a bigger sampling have changed your results? Explain why you think so.

Writing

Have children describe how to assemble a set of tiles two thirds of which are blue.

Extending the Activity

1. Have children prepare a bag of Color Tiles in which the probability of drawing any one of the four colors is one fourth. Have them design an experiment in which they use sampling to compare the theoretical probability with the experimental probability.

Teacher Talk

Where's the Mathematics?

In the first part of this activity, children must assemble an assortment of Color Tiles that is two-thirds blue. Some children may puzzle over this at first, since the total number of tiles to be used is not given; children must determine that number for themselves. Some may select a number of tiles at random to be the total and then try to determine how many of the tiles should be blue. In some cases, the number they select may not be workable—two thirds of that number may not result in a whole number of tiles. This may lead children to think about choosing a number that can be divided evenly into thirds, such as 6, 9, 12, 15, and so forth. They can then separate this number of tiles into three equal piles, using blue tiles for two of the piles and other colors for the third pile.

Some children may make groups of three tiles in which two tiles are blue. They may then fill their bag with several of these groups of tiles. Other children may make three stacks of equal numbers of tiles, making two of the stacks using blue tiles and the third stack using other colors. Children should come to see that the total number of tiles in the bag could be many different numbers. Some children may even recognize that the ratio formed by comparing the number of blue tiles to the total number of tiles in the bag will be equivalent to two thirds in every case.

2. Have children prepare a bag of Color Tiles in which the probability of drawing a blue tile is 0 percent (or 0). Then have them prepare another bag in which the probability of drawing a blue tile is 100 percent (or 1). Tell them to compare their bags with others who have done this problem. Ask them to explain why there may correctly be different numbers of tiles in the various bags.

As children sample tiles from their bags, they compare experimental probability with theoretical probability. If the bag was properly prepared, then theoretically two thirds of the tiles sampled should be blue. As they experiment, however, this may not be the case. In fact, it is likely that after sampling a number of tiles and analyzing their results, children may begin to wonder whether the bag was prepared incorrectly. For example, it is not unlikely that from a bag of Color Tiles in which twenty are blue and ten are red, the first five draws are red. Children may even want to peek into the bag to see if it contains any blue tiles at all! Children should find, however, that the more tiles they sample in their experiment, the more closely their results will resemble the proportions of colors of the tiles in the bag.

Some groups may not be convinced that two thirds of the tiles in their bag are blue if their data does not show that exactly two thirds of their samples produced blue tiles. Their expectation of what should happen may prevent them from allowing for the element of chance involved in experimental probability. Children should recognize that it is likely that their data will not show a ratio that is exactly two-thirds blue, even if the bag of tiles was prepared correctly. However, they should also recognize that the more samples they take, the closer the experimental and theoretical ratios will be.

WHAT HAPPENS TO THE AREA?

- Area
- Looking for patterns
- Spatial reasoning

Getting Ready

What You'll Need

Color Tiles, about 50 per pair

Color Tile grid paper, page 91

Overhead Color Tiles and/or Color Tile grid paper transparency (optional)

Overview

Children use Color Tiles to investigate how changing the length and width of a rectangle affects its area. In this activity, children have the opportunity to:

- ◆ reinforce their concept of area
- ◆ discover that doubling the dimensions of a rectangle quadruples its area
- ◆ investigate informal proof

The Activity

Children may find area by counting tiles or by multiplying the rectangle's width by its length.

You may want to remind children of how to use the edge of a tile for measuring the rectangle's perimeter.

During the On Their Own *activity, make sure that children are clear about the definitions of* double, triple, *and* quadruple. *Also, notice whether children need to be reminded to increase both length and width.*

Introducing

- ◆ Display a 3-by-4 rectangle made from Color Tiles.
- ◆ Ask children to work with a partner to determine both of the dimensions and the area of the rectangle. Remind children that *dimensions* refers to length and width of a figure and that *area* refers to the amount of space.
- ◆ Invite volunteers to present their answers. Confirm that length and width are expressed in linear units and that area is expressed in square units.

On Their Own

Do you think that if you double the length and width of any rectangle, you will also be doubling its area?

- Read the following statements:

    - Doubling the length and width of any rectangle will also double its area.
    - Tripling the length and width of any rectangle will also triple its area.
    - Quadrupling the length and width of any rectangle will also quadruple its area.
    - Halving the length and width of any rectangle will also halve its area.

- Working with a partner, use Color Tiles to build rectangles to investigate the first statement and at least 1 of the other 3 statements.

- Decide for each statement whether it is *always true*, *never true*, or *sometimes true.*

- Record some of the rectangles and label the areas to support your conclusions.

- Be ready to discuss your findings with the class.

The Bigger Picture

Thinking and Sharing

Focusing on one statement at a time, invite children to present their conclusions and to support them with drawings and arguments.

Use prompts such as these to promote class discussion:

- What happened to the areas of the rectangles you built when you doubled (tripled, quadrupled, halved) their length and their width? Explain.

- Do you think what you found applies to all other rectangles? Why?

- Would building two different rectangles and doubling (tripling, quadrupling, halving) their length and width prove your conclusions? Why or why not?

- Does the size of the original rectangle have any effect on how the area grows when the length and the width are doubled? How do you know this?

Writing

Have children reword the original statements they investigated to make them true statements.

Extending the Activity

Have children repeat the activity using cubes. Ask them to investigate what happens to the volume of the cube if its length, width, and height are doubled (tripled, quadrupled, halved).

Where's the Mathematics?

In this activity, children must figure out for themselves how to go about investigating the given statements. This may leave some children confused about where to begin. Since no specific rectangles are given, children soon conclude that they must decide for themselves what size rectangles to work with. This may also lead them to realize that it may be important to gather data on several rectangles of different sizes.

Children may investigate in a variety of ways. Some may visualize the change in size by building the original rectangle and each of the new rectangles with Color Tiles and comparing the number of tiles used in each.

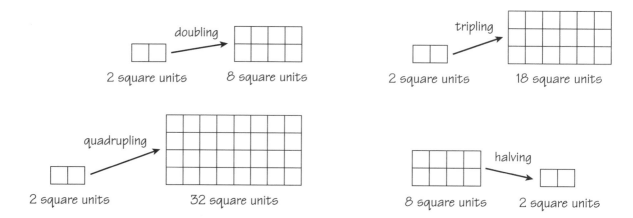

This may help children to conclude that the given statements are not true, or at least not in every case. However, they may not recognize the relationship between the areas; they may not even recognize that any relationship exists. Certainly more rectangles will need to be investigated.

Some children may be content to investigate only until they are convinced that the statements are never true. Others may be curious to examine the data more closely to determine what generalizations (if any) can be made about the effect on the areas. As they build additional rectangles with their Color Tiles and double, triple, quadruple, and halve their dimensions, children may notice a pattern in the changing areas: When the dimensions are doubled, the area is multiplied by 4; when the dimensions are tripled, the area is multiplied by 9; when the dimensions are quadrupled, the area is multiplied by 16; and when the dimensions are halved, the area is one fourth of the original area. Children may recognize that the factors by which the areas increase are perfect squares; in fact, they are the squares of the factors by which the length and width were increased. Although they may or may not be able to explain why this is the case, children may realize that it has something to do with the fact that area is the product of length and width.

Some children may choose to illustrate their findings on grid paper. They may draw the original rectangle, draw the enlarged (or reduced) rectangle, and shade the part of the new rectangle that represents the additional area. Figure B below shows the enlargement of Figure A after its dimensions were doubled. Shading is used to show the "new" units of area.

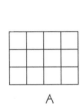

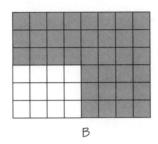

A   B

Drawings may help children determine how the area has grown by enabling them to see how many of the original-size rectangles fit into the new rectangle. For example, when the sides of Figure C below are tripled, they form the rectangle in Figure D, which can be covered with nine rectangles the size of Figure C.

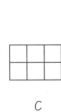

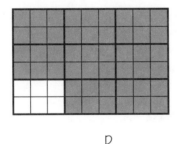

C   D

Some children may think the area has been increased eightfold because there are 8 new rectangles in the area. Clarify that the new rectangle consists of 9 rectangles the size of the original rectangle, and therefore its area is 9 times as big.

Depending on how far they take their investigation, children may or may not discover the factors by which area increases as dimensions increase. They should, however, have explored enough different-sized rectangles to feel confident in asserting that the given statements are never true. Although this investigation does not serve as proof, the experience of investigating to the point of relative certainty is important and meaningful and provides an introduction to the idea of proof in mathematics.

WHAT'S YOUR PREDICTION?

- Sampling
- Organizing and interpreting data
- Predicting

Getting Ready

What You'll Need

Small paper bags, each containing 8 red, 4 blue, and 4 green Color Tiles, 1 per group

Sample bag containing 6 green and 2 yellow tiles

The Activity

It is likely that children will not predict exactly what is in the bag. Let children know that this is okay and that as long as logical reasoning is used, even inexact predictions are valid.

Overview

Children draw Color Tiles from a bag in order to predict how many tiles there are of each color. In this activity, children have the opportunity to:

- experiment with sampling with replacement
- collect and organize data
- use proportional reasoning
- explore the connection between making predictions and the size of a sample

Introducing

- Hold up your sample bag. Tell the class that it contains eight Color Tiles, some green and some yellow. Let children know that without looking into the bag, they are going to predict how many tiles of each color are likely to be in the bag.

- Invite a volunteer to draw a tile from the bag, state its color, and return it to the bag. Repeat this several times with different children while another child keeps track of the number of tiles of each color that are drawn.

- After ten or twelve samples have been taken, ask children if they are ready to make a prediction. If a number of children think they need more data, continue sampling until most children agree that they have enough information. Then ask for predictions, and have children give the reasoning behind each prediction as well.

- Now reveal the contents of your bag and have children verify their predictions.

On Their Own

Can you figure out how many tiles of each color are in a bag of Color Tiles by checking the color of only 1 tile at a time?

- There are 16 Color Tiles in your group's bag. Some are blue, some are red, and some are green.

- Take turns sampling the tiles in the bag. Each time, draw 1 tile from the bag without looking inside. Record the color of the tile, then return it to the bag. Shake the bag to mix the tiles for the next draw.

- Continue sampling until you are ready to predict the number of each color of tile in the bag.

- Write down your group's predictions, the number of each color picked, and the total number of samples you took.

The Bigger Picture

Thinking and Sharing

Call on representatives from each group to give the group's predictions about what was in the bag. Ask how many samples were drawn and how many tiles of each color there were in all. Record this information on the chalkboard. Combine group totals to get class totals.

Use prompts like these to promote class discussion:

- How did you decide when to stop sampling and make your predictions?

- Did you change your predictions at any time? Why or why not?

- How sure were you about your final predictions? Why?

Now combine the group totals to get class totals. Ask children to discuss the class results with their group, and invite them to adjust their predictions if they wish. Record any new predictions next to the original predictions. Finally, allow children to look inside their bags and check their predictions.

- How close were your original predictions to the actual number of tiles of each color in the bag?

- Did you change your predictions after examining the class data? If so, why? Were your new predictions more accurate than your original predictions?

- Do you think there is any connection between the number of tiles sampled and the accuracy of a prediction? Explain.

Extending the Activity

Have children repeat the activity using sixteen or more Color Tiles and two or four colors rather than three.

Where's the Mathematics?

The study of probability deals with making decisions in the face of uncertainty. *What's Your Prediction?* gives children an opportunity to work with this kind of situation. In predicting the contents of a closed bag, children use the recognized technique of *sampling* to learn about the population in which they are interested (in this case, the tiles in the bag). Children are encouraged to draw and replace tiles as many times as they think they need to in order to make predictions. But even after several minutes of sampling, the data on which their predictions are based may not accurately represent the breakdown of tile colors in the bag. After all, it is conceivable that in doing a relatively small sampling, children will not draw certain tiles or will draw the same tiles over and over again.

As children experiment, they naturally apply proportional reasoning to interpret the samples they have drawn. For example, one group, having picked and replaced seven blue, six red, and seven green tiles in twenty draws, might reason that the bag contains about the same number of each color of tile. Another group with different sampling results might reason as follows: "We picked twenty tiles, but didn't pick a single blue. Because we were told that the tiles in the bag were blue, red, and green, the bag must contain only one or two blues. We drew red tiles fourteen times and green tiles six times, so we think there are ten reds, five greens, and one blue in the bag."

In the course of this activity, children can observe that proportional reasoning alone does not ensure the accuracy of predictions based on sampling. In fact, for a prediction to be fairly accurate, proportional reasoning must be applied to a sizable sample. Thus, when groups pool their data, the class totals are likely to show that half of the tiles in the bag are red and that there are equal numbers of blue and green tiles. By comparing individual group results with class totals, children discover for themselves that the large sample is more representative of what is in the bag than are the smaller samples.

Listing each group's results when pooling data allows children to see that the same data can yield different predictions. For example, if the data from 30 draws is 16 red, eight green, and six blue tiles, one group might predict that the bag contains eight red, five green, and three blue tiles, whereas another might claim the bag contains nine red, four green, and three blue tiles. Although neither prediction identifies exactly what is in the bag, both reasonably approximate the proportions of colors based on the given data, and both are valid conclusions. Some children may realize that the proportions will be easier to figure out if the children sample some multiple of the total number of tiles in the bag (16 in this case). That is, if they make 32 draws, they can simply cut their results in half to make predictions for 16 tiles.

Tiles drawn		Totals
Red	﬩﬩ ﬩﬩ ﬩﬩ l	16
Green	﬩﬩ lll	8
Blue	﬩﬩ l	6
Total Sample		30

Listening to classmates describe how they made their predictions and why they chose a particular number of draws helps children see that evidence-based predicting is different from simply guessing. It also gives them a chance to learn how data can be interpreted and how it can be valuable in analyzing situations.

COLOR TILE GRID PAPER

Color Tiles ◆ Grades 5-6 **91**

5-TILE ARRANGEMENTS

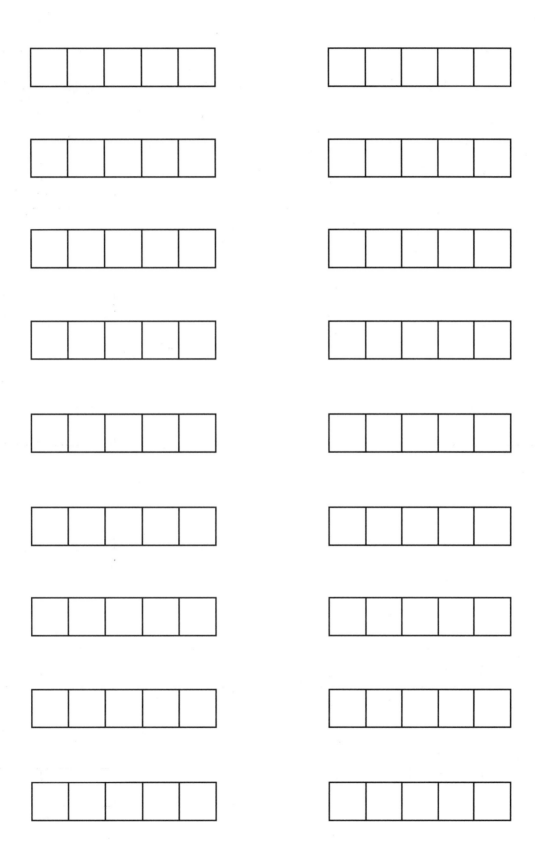